TIME
ANXIETY

OTHER TITLES BY CHRIS GUILLEBEAU

TIME ANXIETY

THE ILLUSION OF
URGENCY AND A
BETTER WAY TO LIVE

Chris Guillebeau

**CROWN
CURRENCY**

New York

CROWN CURRENCY
An imprint of the Crown Publishing Group
A division of Penguin Random House LLC
1745 Broadway
New York, NY 10019
currencybooks.com
penguinrandomhouse.com

Library of Congress Cataloging-in-Publication Data is on file with the publisher.

Hardcover ISBN 978-0-593-79955-0
International edition ISBN 979-82-17-08627-6
Ebook ISBN 978-0-593-79956-7

Editor: Leah Trouwborst | Associate editor: Amy Li | Consulting editor: Talia Krohn | Illustrator: Emily McDowell | Production editor: Terry Deal Text designer: Aubrey Khan | Production: Jessica Heim | Copy editor: Jill Twist | Proofreaders: Daina Penikas and Tess Rossi | Indexer: Jay Kreider Publicist: Tammy Blake | Marketer: Kimberly Lew

Manufactured in the United States of America

9 8 7 6 5 4 3 2 1

First Edition

The authorized representative in the EU for product safety and compliance is Penguin Random House Ireland, Morrison Chambers, 32 Nassau Street, Dublin D02 YH68, Ireland, https://eu-contact.penguin.ie.

FOR DAVID FUGATE

AND

For everyone who worries

about not having enough time

TIME IS RUNNING OUT IN MY LIFE.

THERE'S NOT ENOUGH TIME IN THE DAY.

TIME ANXIETY

The Fear of Running Out of Time

Time is passing me by.
I don't feel in control of my circumstances.
There's something I should be doing,
but I don't know what it is.

This is a book for people who worry about time running out.

It's for those who feel like there's never enough time for the things that matter, who fear they're too late for something important in their life, and who sense there's something they should be doing right now—but aren't sure what it is.

They can't always put their finger on this feeling. They might call it by a name, or they might not call it anything at all. Either way, it never really goes away.

I call this experience *time anxiety*. I didn't come to study it out of academic interest. As I'll share with you, my interest in it started from my own struggle of several years. Before long, I learned that many other people were dealing with time anxiety in their own way—and that most of what they did in an attempt to remedy it was making it worse.

When I wrote a blog post sharing my experience, the comments and emails poured in:

- "My friends and I talk about this all the time."
- "I thought it was just me."

- "I've always felt this way, but never knew there was a name for it."
- "It affects me every single day."
- "Ever since the pandemic, these feelings have intensified."
- "I honestly believe this is the defining problem of my life."

It was clear that this was a serious, understudied problem. As I began paying more attention, I noticed that most people focused on one of two ways of describing it. Their source of feeling unsettled had to do with either their big-picture view of life or the day-to-day challenge of managing it all. And for some lucky people, including me, it was both.

EXISTENTIAL:
TIME IS RUNNING OUT IN MY LIFE.

DAILY ROUTINE:
THERE'S NOT ENOUGH TIME IN THE DAY.

This list of symptoms breaks down the difference between these two forms a bit more:

EXISTENTIAL

- Ruminating on past decisions that "wasted" precious time
- Feeling a heightened sense of pressure to make every moment count, leading to chronic stress

- Worrying that you'll never find your true calling or purpose and that you'll look back on your life with regret
- Experiencing a sense of dread or panic when contemplating the finite nature of life

DAILY ROUTINE

- Putting intense pressure on yourself to complete tasks within a certain time frame
- Feeling like you're always "on" and can't truly disconnect from work, even during your downtime
- Struggling to focus on one task at a time, constantly switching between tasks, or getting distracted by new demands
- Rarely experiencing a sense of completion or satisfaction after finishing a task or meeting a deadline

Those who focused more on the existential, big-picture view would say things like, "I don't know what to do with my life, and it feels like time is running out."

Meanwhile, those who focused on the challenge of a daily routine would say things like, "There's not enough time in the day to do what I need, and I keep falling behind."

Either way, their sense of angst was similar: *Time is passing me by. I don't feel in control of my circumstances. There's something I should be doing, but I don't know what it is.*

People experiencing time anxiety tend to be plagued with indecisiveness. They often voice feelings of frustration around "What should I do next," an open-ended question that can refer to almost anything. The question could be asked about a project, a relationship, or literally anything else in life.

Whether you're facing a big life change or simply trying to decide which task to tackle next, analysis paralysis has a way of taking over your mind. You end up spiraling and consuming energy. Ultimately, you become even more frustrated at your inability to make simple choices.

There was one more thing that came up frequently in these initial comments: *a sense of being too late.* Whether it's an overdue career change, a relationship that should have ended years earlier, or a dream deferred, the internalized belief of missing your chance can be especially painful.

One woman in her late thirties put it this way:

As I get older, the feeling of time passing me by and the feeling of missing my chance at doing certain things has become more prominent. If you factor in the fact that I had little choice of what I did with my time the first 18 years, I should actually have MORE time to do the things I want to do in this second half of my life. But for some reason, it doesn't feel that way.

Later, when I conducted more research, I'd notice something interesting: this worry came up among people of all ages, from fourteen to seventy-four. It's a cross-generational fear! While it's true that some things in life do have a concrete timeline, it seems that the fear of being "too late" isn't always correlated to it.

Even so, when you start to believe you've missed a chance at something important, it doesn't feel good.

Time Anxiety Is More than FOMO and Different From ADHD

The experiences I'm describing are sometimes labeled as FOMO (the fear of missing out), but time anxiety is different. FOMO is focused on the present ("something is happening without me"), whereas time anxiety connects to all three dimensions: the past, present, and future. You feel regretful about the past, uncertain or hesitant about the present, and apprehensive of the future.

PAST: I wish I'd done things differently.

PRESENT: I don't know what to do right now.

FUTURE: I'm worried about what will happen in the days and years to come.

Time anxiety can overlap with neurodivergent conditions like ADHD or autism spectrum disorder, but it also stands on its own. You can be neurotypical (someone with normal brain development) and still struggle with the fear of running out of time, as well as the angst over how to spend it. Alternatively, you can have ADHD, autism, or another condition and find that time anxiety acts as an amplifier of your other behaviors.

Regardless of any specific diagnosis, the struggle with time anxiety deeply affects your ability to plan and complete simple tasks. It leads you to get stuck for hours or days at a time, to under- or overestimate how much time something will take, and to chronically avoid unpleasant situations—even when taking just a few minutes to focus on them would provide immediate relief.

I was diagnosed with ADHD as a child, and I started taking medication for it as an adult. The treatment helped, and so did learning more about the condition. Still, my inability to focus on tasks wasn't the only problem. I also lived in a state of distress, constantly worrying about whether I was doing the right things.

Time anxiety produces a recurring sense of discontent. It's an undercurrent that tells you something isn't right. Sometimes it recedes into the background, but it always comes back.

Productivity "Hacks" Mask the Problem

As I reviewed the research, I started rethinking my approach to how I spent my time. I'd been a lifelong fan of productivity methods, but I gradually grew disillusioned. The more work I finished or the more goals I accomplished, the more that remained. There was never any end to it. Simply adopting new habits or routines, or signing up for more apps and services provided a misleading sense of progress.

Worst of all was a sneaking suspicion that I was getting better and better at doing the wrong things. I was addicted to the dopamine hit of working through lists. Just like any other drug, it felt good at first—but the lasting effects were limited and sometimes even harmful.

At the end of any given day, I finally realized, it didn't matter how many emails I'd responded to or tasks I'd checked off my lists. Magically, more emails appeared! Another set of tasks was always waiting to replace the set I'd finished.

• • •

It's hard to overstate how deeply rooted the gospel of efficiency is in Western culture. Hundreds of books, workshops, seminars, and TED talks reinforce the same false belief structure. Many of them claim to provide definitive answers—even though people with an interest in productivity are generally the first ones to float from method to method.

I used to follow a productivity expert who kept changing the systems he recommended. Every few months he'd get really excited and host a new seminar about his latest method.

In some sense, I knew he was changing his systems because he had something to sell, but it didn't seem like a total act. He was genuinely enthusiastic about whatever the new method was, at least until a new one came along.

Finally, after more than two years of gushing tech recommendations, he sent out a message announcing his newest discovery. This method was totally analog. In a video that accompanied his announcement, he pointed to a paper journal and said, "I've learned that the best way to manage your life has nothing to do with technology; it's all right here in this simple journaling process."

"Wow," I thought, "we've come full circle." Following an array of apps and technical solutions, we're now back to the way people have been writing things down for hundreds of years. After that, I never heard from him again. No doubt he's off being productive somewhere else.

The world of productivity advice, and time management in particular, makes an appealing, impossible promise. It claims to offer order in a world of chaos but fails to equip us with tools that address the root problem. Along the way, it creates other issues of its own, leading us to cycle between feeling ashamed of being able to conquer the beast and gearing up to try one more time.

SOLUTIONS AHEAD

You Have the Power to Feel Better

So what can be done? It turns out that we aren't entirely power-less. As I learned, you first need to approach the problem differently. You need to understand why everything you've tried so far has failed you. You need to rewrite some deeply ingrained patterns.

To be fair, this can be harder than it sounds, at least at first. But I promise it's worth the effort.

In search of answers, I began a series of surveys that more than a thousand people dutifully completed. I mined the results for insights and common themes. I conducted interviews, reviewed academic studies, and tried everything I could on my own, from morning pages to ketamine.

What I found was sometimes frustrating, especially all the unhelpful advice that magnifies the problem. My interpretation of "tips and hacks" shifted from favorable to skeptical to downright hostile. Much of this advice, I saw, did more harm than good. It encouraged the false belief that somehow you can conquer an unconquerable challenge, if only you work extra hard and get up early enough in the morning.

• • •

Other times the investigation surprised me, leading me to question my own long-held assumptions and beliefs. It wasn't just all the other experts who were wrong. I, too, was mistaken. I had committed classic attribution errors, assigning successes to my own brilliance and severely blaming myself for failures.

It turned out I wasn't brilliant or stupid; I'd simply fallen into the trap of believing I could do everything. I'd also based my self-esteem and perceived status on what other people thought of me, another classic error that can only lead to misery.

In turn, this informed my daily operating system, intensifying the sense that I just had to work harder to feel less anxious—even when I was working hard on the wrong things.

It's not just my friend the productivity expert who's been so misled. His experience was an exaggerated version of what I've done, and maybe you have as well.

If you're like me, you tend to get excited about a new habit or method and try it out for a while, but it doesn't really stick. So then you try something else, and the same thing happens. More apps, more journals, more promises to fix everything once and for all—a promise that sets itself up for inevitable failure.

So instead of overpromising, I'll tell you the opposite: this book will not fix everything for you once and for all. It can, however, give you both a new perspective and a toolkit to make life much easier.

My objective is to help you overcome the fear of running out of time, as well as the chronic indecisiveness over how to spend it. I want you to be able to look to the future with hopefulness, not trepidation. I want you to know that it's possible to face busy days with a sense of purpose.

In short, I want to help you *feel better and worry less*.

What You Won't Learn

Another obvious theme from the surveys I conducted: people are fed up with hearing the same kinds of advice about how "doing it all" shouldn't be so difficult.

In the words of one respondent:

I'm so tired of hearing "Beyoncé has the same twenty-four hours a day as you do." Please, for the love of all that is good in this world, people need to stop saying that. Comparing my situation to a wealthy famous person is ridiculous.

I promise to not compare you to Beyoncé, or tell you to keep grinding away at something that isn't helpful and doesn't feel good. I won't suggest you get up at 3:00 a.m. to run a marathon before completing a full day at work, pausing for lunch to write a chapter of your novel.

If you're in charge of childcare or looking after elderly parents, I won't pretend that it's easy to juggle these responsibilities with the other things you want to do. It's not easy. It's hard! The struggle is real.

And yet, the fact remains: you're still burdened with the sense of limited time and the angst of deciding how to spend it. You still want to do more of what matters. You're certain there's something better waiting for you, if only you could figure it out.

That's why you need to do something about this problem. If nothing changes, you'll always feel stuck.

So without holding back and without judgment, we'll take a hard look at the root causes of time anxiety to see how you can feel better even in the midst of life's chaos.

You'll Also Be More Effective

One more thing: even though most productivity methods can do more harm than good, some are helpful when used in the right contexts. By learning a few simple, counterintuitive strategies, you'll likely end up accomplishing more than you did before. This is a by-product of reducing time anxiety, not the main goal—but if you want to be more effective, accomplishing more should happen naturally along the way.

Mostly, though, you'll feel more purposeful and aware of your surroundings.

In one of the final surveys I conducted, I asked respondents this question: "How would it feel to not be anxious about time?"

I received hundreds of responses. Many of them were unique, but many others focused on one of a few common themes:

"I'd be excited about my goals again. I'd look forward to starting my day and planning further ahead."

• • •

"I wouldn't worry so much about doing the wrong thing. I'd be focused and purposeful, and wouldn't have as many false starts."

• • •

"I'd stop getting mad at myself for not having everything figured out. I'd feel more self-confident and able to make better decisions."

• • •

"I'd feel free. I'd finally learn to let go of something that's bothered me for a long time, so I could look to the future with hopefulness."

Consider how you'd answer the following question. Whatever regret you have about the past, whatever worries you have about the future, and whatever frustration you have about the present, what if these feelings receded to the background, leaving you free to proceed with confidence?

However that looks to you, I'll do my best to help you get there. Let's start the first chapter with some things you can do to feel less overwhelmed right now.

CONTENTS

PART 1
Breaking the Stress Cycle

■ **INTERLUDE**

PART 2
Rewriting Time Rules

▓ **INTERLUDE**

PART 3
Owning Your Time

PART 1

Breaking the Stress Cycle

You have the power to overcome time anxiety by challenging the thoughts that keep you trapped. Imagine mastering the moment, discerning what's truly urgent, and accepting the natural limits of time. This section guides you to transform your perspective on time, allowing you to live more fully.

ANXIETY INHIBITS YOUR
ABILITY TO THINK
CLEARLY IN THE
MOMENT.

1

Start by Giving Yourself More Time

BEFORE YOU CAN MAKE BIG DECISIONS
ABOUT YOUR LIFE, YOU NEED TO REDUCE
THE IMMEDIATE PRESSURE YOU FEEL.

When I started writing this book, I first outlined lots of ideas about mortality, leaving a legacy, and how to complete big projects.

We'll come back to some of that later. But as my editor and I poured over the survey results, we realized that <u>time anxiety prevents people from moving forward in some very basic operations of life</u>.

Over and over, readers said things like:

"I get absolutely frozen and can't make simple decisions."

. . .

"I've had the same important task at the top of my to-do list for ten days in a row, but I just can't bring myself to face it."

. . .

"It feels like everyone else understands something very simple that I don't get at all."

They also tended to use absolute terms such as "always," "never," and "constantly" to describe their struggles with time. They've *always* felt this way, they would *never* be better, and they *constantly* felt the pull of wondering if they were spending their time well.

Anxiety inhibits your ability to think clearly in the moment. When you feel anxious, you don't always make rational decisions. Sometimes you know what you should do, but you feel incapable of doing it. Other times, you don't have any idea what you should do—you just know *what you're doing now isn't good.*

Either way, you feel trapped. And when you're trapped, the first step is to locate an escape route.

You would not tell a person experiencing a panic attack that they need to get to work on filing their taxes, break up with their boyfriend, and mail off an overdue rent check. Perhaps they need to do all of those things eventually, but they first need to deal with what feels like an emergency. (And simply telling them to "calm down" probably won't help much.)

They need to learn to address their breathing, lower their heart rate, and understand that even though what they are feeling seems overwhelming, *it will get better.* Only once they're able to do these things will they be able to deal with more systemic problems.

Those actions I mentioned—lowering your heart rate, noticing your breath patterns—are part of regulating your nervous system, the essential part of your body that allows you to do any sort of cognitively intensive work. When this delicate ecosystem is in balance, you're at your best. You're able to make decisions, plan ahead, and manage your emotions with relative ease. Throw in stress or anxiety, however, and suddenly the ecosystem is under threat.

When you're struggling with time anxiety, you need to deal with the immediate symptoms first. One of the reasons why you experience distress is because you perceive a *time shortage* in your life. Therefore, let's help you achieve a *time surplus*, where more time is available to you, even in the midst of a busy life.

I'll show you some strategies for this in the chapters that follow, including:

1. When to do things poorly (Not everything needs to be done with excellence or even done well.)
2. Why not finishing things is perfectly acceptable (Many things can be left undone, often permanently.)
3. How to decide "What is enough?" for any type of project or creative work, so that you always have an end point in mind

But for now, try taking some quick actions that can help you right away. These actions will give you space to make bigger decisions and figure out how you really want to spend your time.

1. Practice "Time Decluttering"

Home-organizing guides often focus on decluttering, the act of removing items from your home or work space that don't have a useful or joyful purpose. It can be a useful habit at times.

But while physical decluttering and improving your environment can help somewhat, time anxiety usually stems from worries in our mind or commitments that occupy our schedule. It's a little different from, "I've got too many socks, so I should pare down."

That's why, in addition to any physical tidying up that you do, look at your calendar for the next few weeks and challenge yourself to remove a few items. Most likely, you can find some upcoming appointments that seemed like a good idea when you added them but now feel less important.

Later I'll show you a concept called rules of engagement that will help you make fewer commitments in the first place, but you can practice time decluttering without any further knowledge.

Go through your schedule and ask, "Do I need to do this thing? Is it serving a purpose in my life? Do I still want to do it?"

See what you can remove, and notice how it feels to reclaim that time as a gift to yourself. It's an easy but powerful way to multiply the time that's available to you in the near future.

ACTION: *Can you clear at least two items from your calendar for the next week?*

2. Put a Brick in Your Inbox

How accessible are you right now? How many people have a direct line to your attention span?

Most of us have multiple "inboxes" where people can reach us. I don't just mean any email inboxes you have, although those certainly count. But in addition, we have voicemail and voice memos, social media profiles that allow for direct messaging, apps with communication features, and more. Then of course, there are work networks (Teams, Slack, WhatsApp, others) that many employees are expected to participate in. For you, there might be something else I haven't mentioned.

Guess what? Being accessible all the time is costly! You can get some of your attention back by stepping away from some of these tools or at least minimizing your use of them.

ACTION: *Think through all the different ways that people can get your attention. Can you turn off at least one of these inboxes?*

I know this feels difficult to some people, including some who believe they simply *can't* lower the level of access they provide to the world. If that's you, understand that you are not powerless. There's something you can do, even if it seems small.

Note: I'm not suggesting that you lessen your availability for anyone who's physically dependent on you, such as young children. In fact, turning off some of your accessibility elsewhere will allow you to be more present for the people you care most about.

One way or another, start resisting the expectation that your attention span is up for grabs. It shouldn't be—it belongs to you, after all.

Notice How It Feels to Give Yourself Time

Taken together, actions like these point to an overall strategy of *giving yourself more time*. Do whatever you can to achieve this result. You could extend the idea even further by:

1. Removing annoying, time-wasting apps from your phone
2. Turning off all but the most essential notifications
3. No longer agreeing to requests and commitments without thinking about them*

As you do this, notice how it feels. Isn't it nice? You've been worried about not having time, and now you are literally giving it back to yourself.

To return to the home-organization example: the items on the list above are like decluttering, but perhaps even more valuable. You didn't just gain more room in your sock drawer—you took back more of the most precious resource in the world!

These practices are not simply "doing less." As you'll see, we all want to do more of some things and less of others. What we're doing here is removing some of the constant pressure you face, so that you can feel more in control of your time and make better decisions moving forward.

Even if it's just an extra twenty minutes that you gain, spend this time however you'd like. Don't automatically assign it to the types of tasks you were doing before you started thinking like this. Use some of it for activities that feel joyful, refreshing, and stimulating. This time belongs to you.

Identity Shift

Finally, I encourage you to <u>begin thinking differently about your relationship with time</u>. What does this mean and how do you do it?

---

* Instead, pause and consider: *Is this really something I want to do? If I agree to the request, what will I be passing up on?*

It means that perhaps you've taken on an identity of "having this problem." This is another common pattern of thinking that came up in my survey results. It's expressed in statements like:

"This is just the way I am."

"I am a person who is always late to meet my friends."

"I will always feel frazzled and overwhelmed."

This type of thinking is not value neutral. It frequently makes things worse, sending you into a spiral of negativity and preventing you from making any real changes.

It might be true that your brain operates differently from other people's—but even if you're neurodivergent, this doesn't mean you are destined to always have the problems you're experiencing now. You just need to approach the problems differently from what you've been doing so far.

The feelings you've had of being crushed and overwhelmed do not need to become a permanent state of being. This is not the only option for you—you can get past it! Things can be better.

We'll build on this more in the next chapter, with an exercise called thought countering. For now, just try thinking of yourself differently than you have before:

"I am a person who is figuring things out."

"I am learning to be more assertive."

"Even though this is hard for me, I'm making progress."

There's more to be done, but this is a good start. Remember, just as it's hard to calm down when you're having a panic attack (even though that is ultimately the goal), it's hard to make big life changes when you feel the pressure of not having enough time or the uncertainty of how to decide on small things.

But this can all be different. You are a person who is learning to be more in control of your life and your time.

Time anxiety prevents you from moving forward in the basic operations of life. When you give yourself the gift of time, you begin a process of feeling more free.

PRACTICE

Overcome Overwhelm by Starting Simply

"I'M SO OVERWHELMED THAT I CAN'T DO ANYTHING."

Have you ever felt that way? There's either so much to do that you struggle in taking it all in, or you don't know where to start, or you experience so much distress in thinking about it that you simply do nothing at all.

When we're overwhelmed, we sometimes freeze and are unable to do much of anything that addresses the problem. We might run or avoid the problem for as long as possible, even with the knowledge that this effort may eventually backfire.

Or, as noted, we simply sit back and do nothing.

To others, this behavior can look like laziness, or even stupidity. (Maybe we've thought this way about someone else, too. Why on earth can't that person make simple progress? The answer is: they would if they knew how.)

The next time you feel overwhelmed, try this:

- **Calm your nervous system.** Take three deep breaths, holding them for a few seconds each before releasing. This helps activate your body's relaxation response. Next, ground yourself by noticing five things in your environment that you can see, helping to bring your focus to the present.*

---

* Some people with sensory sensitivities don't like breathing exercises. Two

- **Reject or reframe catastrophic thinking.** Just as you can learn to rethink the idea of excellence (not everything has to be amazing; some things are just fine being good enough), you can rethink the idea that you're in the midst of a huge disaster. You're just overwhelmed—it happens! You've been here before, and you made it through.
- **Pick one thing you can do, and then do it.** Just one thing! If you need to answer an email, open it and type the first sentence, which is often something simple and low-energy ("Hi there" or "Thanks for the message").

You might not need a huge project-management system to deal with your overwhelm. Instead, it might be better to just take it slow and work through things piece by piece, while also remembering that the concept "do it poorly" is sometimes okay. (We'll develop this idea in more detail later in the book.)

---

alternatives are guided imagery, where you visualize a peaceful and calming scene, and body scanning, where you mentally scan and relax different parts of your body.

The problem with
doing nothing is not
knowing when you
are finished.

—NELSON DeMILLE

ONCE A FAILURE, ALWAYS A FAILURE.
OVER-GENERALIZATION
NOTHING EVER GOES RIGHT FOR ME.
BLACK-AND-WHITE THINKING
I CAME IN SECOND, SO I'M A LOSER.
FILTERING
I MUST HAVE DONE SOMETHING WRONG.
PERSONAL-IZATION

2

Cognitive Distortions

WHEN OUR MIND PLAYS TRICKS ON US,
WE BELIEVE IRRATIONAL THINGS AND BECOME
EVEN MORE ANXIOUS.

Do you ever have recurring, intrusive thoughts? A running narrative in your head that you suspect isn't helpful but just won't leave you alone?

Consider the scenarios below. Don't worry if you don't relate to each aspect of them. Just ask yourself if you can relate to any of them on a broad level:

Alex, a high school junior, misses a question on a practice test for the upcoming SAT and immediately thinks, "I'm going to fail all my exams. I'm just not smart enough for college." This single mistake leads Alex to overgeneralize their entire academic ability and future prospects.

• • •

Dana, a twenty-eight-year-old who recently started a new job, struggles to complete all her tasks within the first few weeks. She gets overwhelmed and is unable to identify which of the requests she receives are truly important. Dana's thinking pattern fails to recognize the learning curve and adjustment period that comes with any new position.

· · ·

Jackson, a single parent, manages to complete most of his daily tasks but runs out of time to make a home-cooked meal, opting for takeout instead. He fixates on this "failure," filtering out all the successes of the day, like helping his son with homework and paying bills on time.

These are all examples of cognitive distortions: irrational or exaggerated thought patterns that can perpetuate the state of time anxiety.

When you're experiencing a distortion, you believe something that isn't real even though this belief often makes the situation worse and then keeps making it worse, becoming a self-destructive loop.

There are different types of cognitive distortions, including:

1. **Overgeneralization**: Seeing one bad outcome as a never-ending pattern of failure
2. **Black-and-white thinking**: Viewing situations in extreme, either/or terms, with no middle ground
3. **Filtering**: Focusing only on the negative details of a situation while ignoring the positive aspects
4. **Personalization**: Thinking everything bad that happens is directly your fault

A young child might experience *personalization* like this:

My friend had a birthday party this weekend, and I wasn't invited. It must be because no one likes me. Maybe I'm just not fun to be around, and that's why I didn't get invited. It feels like I'll never be invited to anything ever again. It's probably better if I just don't have any friends, so I don't have to feel left out.

A twelve-year-old might experience *black-and-white thinking* like this:

I tried out for the basketball team and didn't make it. This means I'm totally useless at sports, doesn't it? No matter how much I practice, I'll never be good enough. Maybe I should just give up on playing sports altogether. It's clear I'm not cut out for this, and everyone's going to remember me as the one who couldn't make the team.

An adult going through a divorce might experience *overgeneralization* like this:

This divorce proves I'm unlovable and always will be. If I couldn't make this marriage work, it's unlikely anyone else will ever want to be with me. I'm doomed to be alone forever.

Everything Is Ruined

A specific type of cognitive distortion, *catastrophizing*, can be particularly debilitating. It involves expecting the worst possible outcome in a situation or viewing an event as far more disastrous than it actually is.

When you catastrophize, you assume worst-case scenarios. You forget someone's name, so you think you have dementia. You're afraid to go hiking, because that's when you'll be attacked by bears. Disaster lies around every corner.

You also tend to experience these scenarios repeatedly in your mind. You fixate, worry, and ruminate.

All of these actions make the situation worse, because it's not just that a bad thing will happen, it's that the bad thing *has already happened* in your mind, and then it happens over and over (and over and over . . .). Remember that time anxiety affects us in all three dimensions of time: past, present, and future. When catastrophizing, it might look something like this:

PAST: I made a terrible, horrible mistake.

PRESENT: Only a very stupid person would make this kind of mistake.

FUTURE: I will never recover from this mistake.

Cognitive distortions often breed shame and low self-worth, which in turn fuel our fear of running out of time. When we believe we're fundamentally flawed or permanently "behind," we're more likely to:

- **Overcommit** while trying to prove our worth to others
- **Procrastinate** on important tasks and goals, having already decided in our minds that we're going to fail
- **Neglect self-care,** believing we don't deserve rest or relaxation until we've "caught up"

Strategies and Solutions

Many of the strategies you'll learn in this book will help you mitigate the effects of cognitive distortions, especially as they relate to the fear of running out of time. For example, you'll be able to do better work if you combine sessions of hyperfocus with sessions of recovery. You'll be able to keep better track of time by making it visual, such as by keeping a colorful timer on your desk.

If you're seeking therapy and want to focus on this area, you'll want to look for someone who specializes in cognitive behavioral therapy, dialectical behavior therapy, or a similar approach.

Outside of formal settings, you can simply start with the understanding that cognitive distortions are exactly what they sound like. These beliefs aren't based on reality! They are untrue and unhelpful.

• • •

As part of labeling the intrusive thoughts, consider a counternarrative. Remind yourself of past successes. If the cognitive distortion leads you to feel like you've lost at something, think about a time in which you won. Inevitably, life consists of both joy and sadness. Sometimes you're up, sometimes you're down.

You could also remind yourself that in those times when you feel bad, there's a way out. Were you ever hurt before? Did you turn out to be okay? Well, one way or another, you'll probably be okay again this time.

Sometimes it helps to point out how silly catastrophic thinking can be, like in some of the examples I used in this chapter. (I don't mean that you're silly for thinking this way, because we all do it. I just mean that the thought patterns can get way out of control.)

An argument with a partner doesn't mean you're going to break up. A breakup doesn't mean you'll never love or be loved again. Losing your job, while stressful, is sometimes the best thing to happen to many people who go on to do something else much more worthwhile.

In fact, with the right reframing of a negative experience, you can even emerge stronger than you were before the experience. Just imagine: the pain of rejection or otherwise falling short can be part of a better you in the future.

When it comes to time anxiety, you'll discover that time does not need to feel so constrictive or overbearing.

Cognitive distortions are powerful illusions that contribute to our anxiety and negative self-worth. We can reduce their effects by labeling them and considering different stories.

PRACTICE

Thought Countering

CHALLENGE AND REPLACE IRRATIONAL THINKING
WITH RATIONAL PERSPECTIVES.

Cognitive distortions can sneak into our minds and make us believe irrational things, increasing our anxiety and stress. Thought countering is a technique to challenge these unhelpful thoughts and replace them with more rational, balanced ones.

1. Identify a Negative Thought

Throughout your day, pay attention to any negative or anxious thoughts that arise, especially as they relate to time. Write down one thought that stands out and seems particularly distressing. For example, you might think, "I'm going to fail this project because I missed a deadline."

2. Label the Cognitive Distortion

Look at your thought and identify the type of cognitive distortion it represents. Is it overgeneralization, black-and-white thinking, or catastrophizing? Labeling the distortion helps you see the irrational pattern. (If you can't decide, don't worry too much about the distinction. Cognitive-distortion types often overlap.)

3. Challenge the Thought

Ask yourself a few questions to challenge the validity of the thought:

1. Is this thought based on facts or assumptions?
2. What evidence do I have that this thought is true or false?
3. Have I faced similar situations before, and if I have, what was the outcome?

4. Create a Counterstatement

Based on your answers, write a rational counterstatement that provides a balanced perspective. For instance, counter "I'm going to fail this project because I missed a deadline" with "I've met deadlines before and can still succeed. What can I do to meet this deadline?" (Or, alternatively, "Missing one deadline doesn't mean I'll fail the entire project. Some deadlines get missed, and that's okay.")

By challenging and countering your irrational thoughts, you can reduce their impact and begin to think in a more realistic way. This practice helps diminish time anxiety and supports a healthier, more positive mindset.

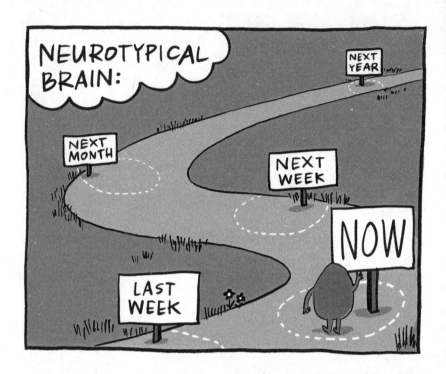
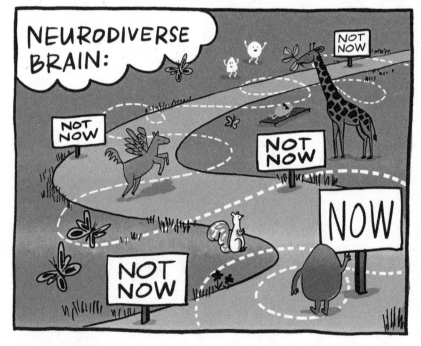

3

Time Blindness Hinders
Your Sense of Time

A CONDITION KNOWN AS TIME BLINDNESS MEANS THAT
YOUR BRAIN PROCESSES TIME DIFFERENTLY, MAKING
IT TRICKY TO PLAN AHEAD OR GAUGE HOW LONG
THINGS TAKE.

Consider these scenarios:

You think you have plenty of time for a work project but then realize that the task is much larger than expected. You begin to panic, and it becomes even harder to focus on what needs to happen.

. . .

You're having so much fun playing a game you don't notice that hours have gone by. Now it's late, and you still have a bunch of other things to do.

. . .

As a busy parent, you often feel like you're racing against the clock. Mornings are chaotic as you try to get small humans ready while preparing for the rest of your day. As the hours pass from morning to night, you feel perpetually behind schedule.

. . .

Your friends have learned that you're always late to meet them, even when you try to be early. It's kind of a joke and kind of not. You want to be more reliable, both as a friend and because being late stresses you out—but you always end up being thwarted by something that comes up along the way.

If you frequently struggle with losing track of time, or if you often underestimate the amount of time required for tasks, you might be experiencing time blindness. The name of this concept comes from a study in the journal *Neuropsychology*. It focused on teenagers with ADHD, and the results showed that these teenagers experienced difficulties with time at a greater rate than a control group.

In short, time blindness refers to chronically misjudging the time you have, often leading to lateness, procrastination, or anxiety about all the things you haven't done. You don't estimate time well, even when you promise yourself you'll do better in the future, and this causes all kinds of other problems.

Time Blindness Means That You Process Time Differently

Time blindness doesn't mean you are careless or irresponsible. It just means that you process time differently.

No one would say that a blind person is careless. We understand that the blind have a real physical limitation, and in fact they probably have to work harder than sighted people to pay attention to their surroundings.

As the original study indicated, time blindness is especially common for people with conditions like ADHD, as well as anyone who's experienced trauma. Even if you're not diagnosed with a specific condition, however, you could still experience time blindness. The disruption caused by a global pandemic caused a lot of us to struggle in different ways. The nonstop cycle of news and social media also impacts our ability to keep up with time.

Whatever the reason, if you struggle with losing track of time, here's a key point:

The more *time blindness* you have, the more *time anxiety* you will experience.

When you don't have a good handle on time, you worry about it. You're constantly rushing without ever feeling settled.

What Can We Do About It?

While time blindness is frustrating, once you understand you're prone to under- or overestimating the amount of time something requires, or that you can easily lose track of time's passing, a few changes in your work and life patterns can mitigate the effects.

The first recommendation below is the most important. The others provide tips and examples of how to implement it.

1. Make time more visible in your home and work area.

Don't try to keep track of time in your head. You have plenty of other things to think about, and your working memory is a poor use of timekeeping. In fact, there are these things called "clocks" that can do a much better job!

Your home isn't a casino, where the owners hide all the clocks to keep people from thinking about the time. Put clocks in multiple locations, ideally in every room of the house and in a place where you'll notice them.

You might want to set your computer screensaver to display the time, so that it's the first thing you notice when you return to it after an absence. This doesn't mean you should be constantly checking the time—the purpose of this practice is that a visual reminder of time is easily available to you.

However you choose to do it, *make time more visible*. This will help with the first part of time blindness, where you constantly find yourself losing track of time.

(Note: An exception might be if there's an area of your home where you don't want to be reminded of time, like your bedroom at night or an area where you go strictly to relax. But pretty much everywhere else, frequent time reminders are helpful.)

2. Use timers, alarms, and calendars as your working memory.

In addition to clocks, timers and calendars are your friends. Consider creating visual schedules or lists with clear time blocks for each task or activity.

Set multiple alarms, including one that reminds you well in advance when you need to leave to be somewhere else. Your phone has a built-in alarm app, of course, but you may also want a cheap timer-and-alarm combo to keep on your desk. (You can choose from a range of options online for $15 or less.)

Again, keeping track of time in your head is almost always a mistake. You'll likely misjudge it one way or another. Even if you get the time right, you'll have spent energy you could have used elsewhere.

The solution: put timekeeping on autopilot whenever possible.

3. Make timekeeping sensory or multidimensional.

People who experience a lot of time anxiety tend to have especially strong sensory responses, both positive and negative. When you're dealing with time blindness, anything you can do to reinforce good habits in a way that feels fun will be helpful.

A few ideas in this fashion:

Create playlists of a certain length for different activities (for example, a thirty-minute playlist for a workout, or a fifteen-minute playlist for morning preparation). The end of the playlist serves as an auditory cue that time is up.

Use visual timers instead of, or in addition to, traditional ones. If clocks are stressful, use another type of time keeper! Lots of timers come in fun colors now—I have one on my desk in "dreamsicle orange." These products are sometimes marketed for kids, but they're helpful for adults, too. Search on Amazon or another retailer for "visual timers" or "visual timers for kids" to find a wide selection.

Get creative. I found this example from an ADHD forum on Reddit: "When I do my hair, I play music. I know by the number of songs how long it's taken up. This seems weird because I have a clock in the bathroom, but somehow the music makes more sense to me."

I love creative solutions like that. Find what works for you!

4. Notice "time sucks"—the activities that you chronically underestimate and always end up taking lots of time.

The second way that time blindness shows up is in the difficulty in estimating how long a task takes to complete. For that, it helps to pay attention to "time sucks": activities or habits that consume a disproportionate amount of our time without offering equivalent value in return. Whenever possible, these are activities we want to minimize or eliminate. When we can't cut them out, we need to allocate more time to them on the front end.

Because I'm self-employed, it takes me a while to gather everything I need to work on my taxes. I also have to do work on them more than once a year, since my business structure requires quarterly updates. Even though I work with a wonderful accountant who does the filing, there are still a lot of tasks that only I can do.

I've learned that gathering forms and clarifying expenses is rarely a quick task—yet this is something I eventually have to do. Now whenever tax updates are required, I block out two full hours to work on my side of things. If I have extra time to spare after I'm done, great! But if I don't, I'm not stressed about leaving the task half-finished or cutting something else short.

5. Notice how you procrastinate when you have more time than you expected.

Another kind of time blindness can work in your favor, but only once you understand it. This is where a task doesn't take long to complete, but you *think* it will, so you overestimate the allotted time. Then, you put it off for as long as possible, until you really need to work on it.

Productive, hardworking students sometimes develop this pattern, which can lead to a false reinforcement of procrastination as a viable strategy.

Here's how one of them explained it in a note to me:

> *I think it will take me an hour to prepare for this assignment, but then I procrastinate for forty minutes. It turns out to only take ten minutes to prepare, so I finish with time to spare.*

So in this situation, we have the opposite of the tax-preparing task (which always takes longer than expected). It might be that the real issue is avoidance or dread, something that we'll look at more in another chapter.

One trick here is when you catch yourself thinking, "Ugh, this will take ages," that's your cue to challenge the thought. Maybe give that dreaded task a go and see how long it really takes.

. . .

The negative effects of time blindness will be minimized as you make time more visible in your daily life. And by challenging your tendency to under- or overestimate task durations, you'll get better at starting and finishing with less stress.

Finally, one more recommendation that I'll return to throughout the book: whatever you're doing, *do one thing at a time*. Do it with intention and purpose before turning to something else.

Whenever you can do that, you'll feel more focused on the task at hand—and maybe less pressured about any other things waiting to be done.

Time blindness is a cognitive distortion that causes you to be late, attempt too many tasks, and generally feel frantic or out of control.

PRACTICE

Allow More Time than You Think You Need

LEAVE TEN TO FIFTEEN MINUTES EARLIER
FOR EVERY APPOINTMENT.

You know how you try to do one more thing before you run out the door—and then you end up being late?

Even when you arrive on time, you're often *worried* about not making it. You end up rushing, putting yourself together on the go, and showing up at your appointment feeling flustered—instead of calm and ready for whatever should happen.

I do it too, though I'm learning not to.

The problem is that you are often wrong about how much time you need—and it's not always your fault, but you still end up being late. Traffic or public transit takes a few extra minutes. You didn't account for the waiting time required for elevators, crosswalks, or parking. And even if the appointment is virtual, there are still tasks required to set up and get ready.

The way to preempt all of these problems (or at least many of them) is simple: *allow more time than you think you need*. It's easy! At least when you make yourself do it.

How much extra time is enough? Ten to fifteen minutes is a general rule. Worst case scenario, you're a little early to an appointment. Bring a book.

Resist the urge to cram in one more thing before you move on. Allowing more time than you think you need makes everything better.

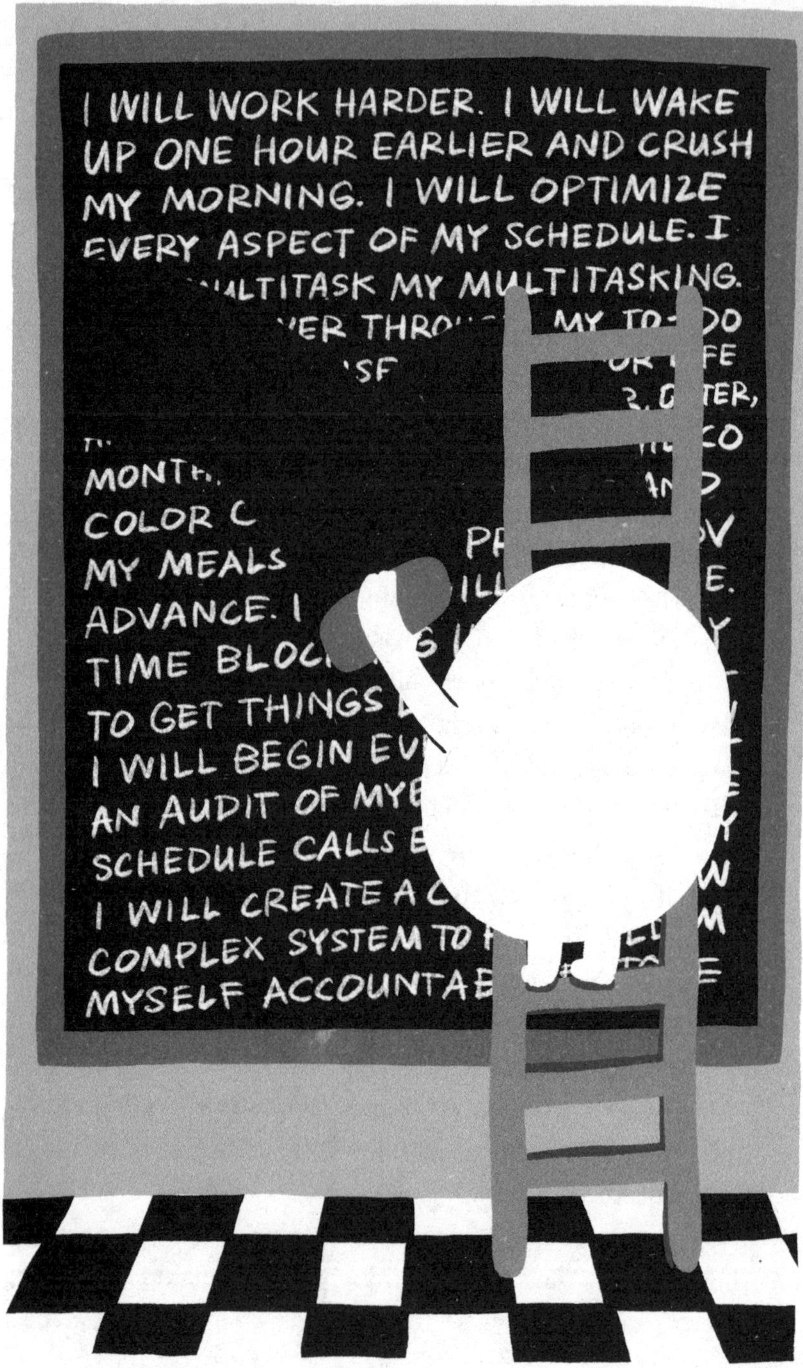

I WILL WORK HARDER. I WILL WAKE
UP ONE HOUR EARLIER AND CRUSH
MY MORNING. I WILL OPTIMIZE
EVERY ASPECT OF MY SCHEDULE. I
ULTITASK MY MULTITASKING.
MY MEALS
ADVANCE. I
TIME BLOC
TO GET THINGS
I WILL BEGIN EV
AN AUDIT OF MY
SCHEDULE CALLS
I WILL CREATE A
COMPLEX SYSTEM TO
MYSELF ACCOUNTAB

4

Unlearning

IF YOU STRUGGLE WITH TIME ANXIETY, SOMEWHERE ALONG THE WAY YOU MIGHT HAVE BEEN GIVEN SOME UNHELPFUL ADVICE. TAKE NOTE OF THESE COMMON SUGGESTIONS, <u>SO THAT YOU CAN IGNORE THEM IN THE FUTURE</u>.

Think about this question:

What is the opposite of learning?

"Forgetting" is the most straightforward answer, but forgetting is similar to breathing. It's often an involuntary process: you forget your keys when you leave the house, or you forget random facts you had to memorize for a test at one point.

For our purposes, a better opposite of learning is *unlearning*.

Unlearning involves the deliberate process of discarding previously acquired knowledge, beliefs, or behaviors. Unlike forgetting, unlearning is a conscious reevaluation of former understandings, making space for new information.

Forgetting is passive, unlearning is active.

Unlearning something can be just as helpful as learning. For example, some people with dyslexia or another learning disability assume that they'll always struggle with reading and should just give up. My friend Karelia told me that she stopped reading books as an adult for years. This was true even though she loved learning, so she felt sad about it. She recently discovered audio-books and had been binge-listening new books every week.

Audiobooks have been around for a while, of course. But Karelia said that at some point she'd internalized the incorrect belief that listening to a book "didn't count" as reading and was something to be ashamed of.

As an author, I feel comfortable telling you: there's nothing wrong with audiobooks! Or ebooks, or anything else that helps you learn. Once Karelia understood her belief about audiobooks was incorrect, her life got better.

In short, unlearning is important if you want to change, grow, or just improve. So when it comes to time anxiety, what do you need to unlearn?

"Just Prioritize" and Other Bad Advice

Even though you weren't taught much about time, you may have received some generic advice along the way. And if time has been a struggle for you, then the odds are even greater that you've encountered this (bad) generic advice.

The first thing on the list is usually: "Set priorities," or per-haps "Learn to prioritize better."

• PRIORITIZE •

• STOP BEING DISTRACTED •

• DON'T WORRY •

I'm guessing that you've heard some version of "the priori-ties talk." But what, exactly, does it mean? Is there a hierarchy to priorities? What do you do about competing priorities? And what do you do when other people's priorities invade your own?

Simply making a list of your top priorities does not get you very far. Inevitably, you end up back where you started: trying to determine how to "fit it all in" and wondering if you're really working on the right things to start with.

Another suggestion you might hear is "Avoid distractions."

Sure, okay—but how's that going? Everyone is distracted, all the time. We can (and should) work to eliminate as many distractions as possible. This will help somewhat. But just like prioritization, being less distracted does not remove time anxiety.

Along with these general observations, you might also be familiar with some specific recommendations, perhaps from well-meaning people—or maybe these are ideas that you've tried to push yourself into at some point:

"Get up one hour earlier and work harder."

Countless motivational videos and bestselling books push this message, which works for about two days. Then, you discover that your body really does need to sleep a certain number of hours almost every night. Sleep deprivation is not a sustainable strategy for anything except more anxiety.

Also, what if you're already getting up early and working hard? One author I know gave me the enraging advice to get up even earlier. "Five a.m. is just not enough these days," he said in a talk. By this logic, I wondered, why should we even sleep at all? Pretty soon this guy would be going to bed at midnight and waking up at 1:00 a.m. every day—if such a thing were humanly possible.

"Fully schedule your life, down to fifteen-minute increments throughout the day."

Having a tight schedule is helpful for some people. Many other people work much better with flexible schedules that accommodate their specific energy levels, environment, and capacity for stimulation.

Overscheduling can also be an avoidance strategy for high achievers, something we'll look at a bit later. When you're too busy to think about your life, you're able to put off proactive decisions under the guise of responding to what seems urgent. You think you're doing all the right things, but really you're just keeping busy.

"Hire a virtual assistant and start outsourcing your unwanted tasks."

What, so now you'll have something else to manage and worry about? I can no longer count the number of people I've heard from who've tried this advice and have come away feeling like failures.

Another problem with outsourcing: time anxiety doesn't just come from the things you don't want to do (and would, therefore, love to hand off to someone else). It also comes from the many different, conflicting things you *want* to do.

"Stop being lazy."

News flash: you're probably not lazy, even if you think you are. Most likely, you struggle with executive functions (initiating tasks, planning, focusing). You need to learn skills, not just stop being "lazy."

What you call being lazy is also a strategy of *learned helplessness*. This is a psychological condition where an individual feels powerless to change their situation due to repeated exposure to unpleasant events. Simply put, **when you don't feel like you're in control of something, you stop trying to change the situation— even when change is possible.**

For example, if you're a teacher, you might continuously grade papers late into the night. This leaves you exhausted and resentful, but you simply don't have the time or energy to consider another way of working, like giving more self-grading assignments.

Finally, you might be able to hyperfocus on some tasks, which is great—but it also leaves you feeling very tired and unable to tackle what seem like simple or easy tasks. This has nothing to do with being lazy.

LAZY
A. LACKING SUPPORT
B. UNDEVELOPED EXECUTIVE FUNCTIONING SKILLS
C. NEGATIVE SELF-TALK
D. FRICTION LOOPS

What Got You Here Won't Take You There

When I started going to therapy, I was the typical client who'd never thought about getting help until I was experiencing a particularly dark period in my life. I couldn't see a way out, and the situation felt hopeless.

The therapist listened to my story, asking questions without providing much feedback. Finally, I had to ask: "So what do you think?" Clearly, I was seeking her approval. I wanted to know what percentile of ability I was in, compared to her other clients. I wanted a grade, maybe even a gold star.

She paused. "It sounds like you've got a lot of skills," she said tactfully. "But what you need to work through now is different. These problems aren't like what you've faced before, so you need to learn new skills."

I didn't get the gold star, but in that very first session I learned an important lesson: *what brought me to that point in my life wasn't sufficient to take me where I needed to go next.* I couldn't just work harder. I couldn't expect the universe to bend to accommodate my will.

That was the start of a whole new process for me. I had a lot to learn, but knowing that I had to approach things differently was immensely helpful.

When we encounter a problem, it's only natural that we try to solve it the same way we've solved other challenges— even if what feels natural isn't the right solution. As the saying goes, if you have a hammer, everything looks like a nail. For example:

- If you're a high achiever who likes to be productive, you try to work harder.
- If you're more laid-back, relaxed, or spiritual, you tend to stop trying and opt out.
- If you tend to avoid difficult situations, you'll procrastinate or divert your attention.
- If your instinct is to freeze, that's what you'll do—and then overthink without taking action.
- If you're a people pleaser, you'll continue to prioritize others' time over your own.

None of these approaches end up helping much with time anxiety. Working hard on the wrong things just leads to frustration—this was a key lesson I had to learn. On the other hand, giving up and opting out (or simply freezing) leads to regret and more questioning. Years later, you'll wonder: What if there was a way forward that I just didn't see?

Either way, you need new tools. When dealing with time anxiety, you have to remember: *what got you here won't get you there.*

Unlearn Something Unhelpful

Unlearning unhelpful advice and reframing it in a way that works better for you can significantly reduce time anxiety. Start by identifying one piece of conventional time-management advice that hasn't worked for you.

You might already have something in mind, but here are a few examples of advice that are generally *unhelpful*:

- "Stick to a rigid schedule."
- "Eliminate all nonessential tasks."
- "Use every spare minute productively."

Next, consider why this advice has been unhelpful for you. The answer might be obvious, or it might require some thought.

Finally, reword the advice into something more helpful. For example:

- "Create a flexible routine." Plan your day with flexible time blocks that can adapt to how you feel and what you need to accomplish.

- "Balance essential and enjoyable tasks." Include tasks that bring joy and mental health benefits, even if they seem nonessential.
- "Value downtime and rest." Recognize the importance of rest and leisure, in addition to work and other things you need to do.

By actively challenging and replacing one piece of advice at a time, you can develop a more supportive approach to how you make decisions about your time.

As you can see, time anxiety is a common problem with many unhelpful proposed solutions. The ones I mentioned are just part of an abridged list—perhaps you can think of something else you've been told that was well-meaning, yet unhelpful in practice. The complete list could go on and on, depending on lots of factors including how you grew up, your job or industry, and what kind of experts or social media you follow.

You might also understand that it's not helpful to keep doing the same things while expecting different results. As you unlearn the unhelpful advice, you also have to treat the problem the right way.

· · ·

The last thing to know for now is that nothing will change unless you do. It's easy to put things off if you're in the midst of a particularly intense season. But when you say that you'll solve this problem later, ask yourself, "Will I, really?"

If you're like me, there will always be another thing that comes along. Time anxiety does not magically get better. Also, if there's one thing that people with time anxiety have in common, it's that we tend to be very good at procrastinating. In the next chapter, we'll consider "time rules" that have been unhelpful to you. Then, you'll create new rules to better serve your needs.

Fortunately, it's possible to unlearn some of the unhelpful lessons you may have absorbed along the way. Unlearning allows you to feel better and achieve more, all by rethinking your relationship with time.

PRACTICE

Unmasking Time Anxiety Traps

EXPLORE HOW YOUR REACTIONS TO FEELING POWERLESS MIGHT BE INTENSIFYING YOUR SENSE OF DISTRESS.

Sometimes, in our attempts to manage time and please others, we inadvertently make choices that worsen our time anxiety. This short reflection aims to help you identify these patterns.

Take a few minutes to consider the following questions. Be honest with yourself—there are no right or wrong answers here.

1. In the past week, how many times did you say yes to something when you really wanted to say no?

- What were you afraid would happen if you declined?
- How did saying "yes" impact your time and stress levels?

2. Think about a recent instance when you chose to do a less urgent task (like organizing your closet) over a more important one (like making a doctor's appointment).

- What emotions were you feeling when you made this choice?
- What thoughts were going through your mind?

3. Are there any recurring tasks in your life that you spend far more time on than necessary?

- Why do you think you haven't found a quicker way to do these tasks?
- What would it feel like to approach these tasks differently?

Awareness is the first step toward change. By recognizing these patterns, you're already on your way to developing a healthier relationship with time.

5

Time Rules Exist to Serve You (You Don't Exist to Serve Time Rules)

WE ALL FOLLOW A SERIES OF "TIME RULES"
AND SELF-IMPOSED RESTRICTIONS.
SOME ARE HELPFUL, WHILE OTHERS ARE NOT.

Without ever thinking about it, you may be living your life by a series of "time rules." These are rules you either set for yourself or rules that are present in the culture you live and work in.

Time rules govern how you spend your time. These rules are often unwritten, but they become deeply embedded in daily life, affecting all sorts of decisions.

Let's start with a simple one: *punctuality*. The definition of "being on time" varies considerably depending on context and circumstance.

For several years in my twenties I lived on board a hospital ship deployed in West Africa. During that time, I learned how different the concept of coordinating a meeting time could be, especially in rural areas. "Village time" could mean a meeting would start thirty minutes, an hour, or even farther out than the scheduled time. Sometimes, the cultural difference in interpreting time led to conflicts and confusion.

Or take mealtimes. When is "dinnertime"? Some people eat whenever they feel like it, but in other households, dinner is served at a certain time. Eating before or after a limited time range is discouraged, sometimes even punished.

Unless you've moved abroad, married into a family structure different from your family of origin, or otherwise made a big lifestyle change, most likely the time that you think of as dinnertime is closely related to what you experienced growing up.

Personal Time Rules

The previous pages have showed examples of societal time rules. You may also have personal time rules, ones that you've set for yourself either intentionally or subconsciously.

Some common ones include:

"I must wake up at 6:00 a.m. every day to be productive."

"I can't start my workday without completing my morning routine."

"I return phone calls within an hour."

"I reply to every email the same day it was sent, without exception."

"If I start a project, I always see it through."

"I can't go to bed until I've completed everything on my to-do list."

While laudable, rules like these can be taken to an unhealthy extreme. I know someone who joined a work conference call from the hospital several hours after giving birth that morning. (She later conceded this was a poor choice.)

I also know multiple people who've become completely

burned out in trying to live up to the high standards they've set for themselves.

Other problems include excessive rigidity—the unwillingness to break or modify a rule even when doing so would be better for you—and monitoring the clock so obsessively that you can't relax in the present, much less be productive.

Taken together, these time rules reflect an all-or-nothing perspective that is doomed to fail. As noted, this approach can lead to an obsession with productivity routines, "digital detoxes," and other stratagems that inevitably fall short.

But of course, there's a better way.

~~I ALWAYS TURN OFF MY PHONE BY 10 P.M.~~

MORE OFTEN THAN NOT,
I TURN OFF MY PHONE BY 10 P.M.

Reframing Time Rules

Start by identifying the time rules that currently shape your daily life. These rules can be personal, such as "I must reply to every email the same day it was sent," or societal, like the expectations around punctuality or mealtimes.

Once you've identified your time rules, ask yourself the following questions for each rule:

1. Does this rule serve my well-being and align with my values? (If not, can I reframe it?)

2. Is this rule overly rigid or inflexible, causing stress or
    anxiety when not followed perfectly?
3. What would happen if I broke or modified this rule?

For example, if you have a personal rule of "I must always see
a project through to completion," you might reframe it as "I will
give myself permission to reassess and adjust my commitments
as needed."

Next, create a set of new time rules that reflect your desired
relationship with time. These rules should be flexible, which
will allow for grace and self-compassion when life inevitably
deviates from the plan. Also, they should be focused on your
well-being rather than rigid productivity. Some examples might
include:

- I will prioritize self-care and rest, recognizing that
  downtime is essential for my well-being and
  productivity.
- I will set realistic expectations for myself and others,
  acknowledging that perfectionism is not always
  necessary or achievable.
- I will practice mindfulness and presence, focusing on
  the task at hand rather than constantly worrying about
  the future or dwelling on the past.
- I will regularly reassess my commitments and priorities,
  making adjustments as needed to ensure alignment
  with my values and goals.

Remember, these new time rules are meant to serve you, not
the other way around. By reframing your time rules, you can

shift your perception of time from scarcity to abundance, culti-
vating a more positive relationship with time and enabling a
more present and purposeful life.

Time Rules Need To Be Helpful, or You Shouldn't Have Them

In addition to reframing existing rules, you may want to make
some new time rules of your own. One possibility comes from
the chapter on time blindness: "Allow more time than you think
you'll need."

In a moment, I'll list some more time rules that might be helpful to you. However, I put the most important part of this chapter right in the title: *Time rules exist to serve you. You don't
exist to serve time rules.*

What this means is that time rules should make your life easier or better somehow. If they make your life harder, you should
drop or change them.

With that disclaimer in mind, here are some suggested time
rules.

- **Establish a time that your phone goes to bed.** Usually,
  this is recommended to be at least two hours before you
  plan to sleep—but if that seems like a stretch, start
  with one hour. Set your alarm, put your phone in its
  charging home, and wish it a good night's rest.
- **Decide in advance how you'll spend most of your time
  at work.** Identify a maximum of three priorities for any
  workday. If much of your day will be taken up by
  meetings or other scheduled obligations, choose a
  maximum of two.

- **Go for a walk for at least fifteen minutes first thing in the morning.** Many dog owners have this habit built in to their routines—so if you don't happen to have a dog, walk an imaginary pet of your choice to get the day started.
- **Decide on certain times a day for checking and responding to messages,** instead of constantly trying to triage. Turn off most notifications whenever possible.
- **Establish clear boundaries for transitions,** such as moving from one project to another, or from a work activity to downtime. (Just like allowing more time than you think you'll need for appointments is helpful, transitions tend to take longer than we expect.)

Many time rules work well with *habit stacking,* a concept that suggests we are more likely to form lasting habits if they build upon one other. For example, when you plan for more transition time, you'll feel less rushed—and then you'll be able to pay closer attention to whatever you should be doing next.

Remember, if you become highly rigid with these rules, they may not always be helpful. Time rules exist to serve you; you don't exist to serve time rules. When the rules are no longer working well, you need new rules.

PRACTICE

How Valuable Were Your Last Forty Minutes?

A SIMPLE WAY TO WASTE LESS TIME—
EITHER YOURS OR ANYONE ELSE'S.

At any point during the day, stop and ask yourself a simple question: "How did I spend my last forty minutes?" Then consider if the past block of time has been useful, productive, or interesting.

- Did you learn something?
- Did you help someone?
- Did you have fun?
- Did you make progress toward one of your goals?

If you have an obvious answer, great. If you don't, it might be helpful to adjust and do something else. What would be a better use of your time for the next forty minutes?

Note that "valuable" can mean a lot of things. This isn't just about being more productive! It's valuable to relax, or to spend time with your kids or a friend.

However you define valuable, try to increase the proportion of value in your life.

**Unlike other forms
of psychological
disorders, the core
issue in trauma is reality.**

—BESSEL VAN DER KOLK

SUBJECT:
Checking In
Third Request
Trying to reach you...
Pls respond ASAP
FW: Hello?!?
ACTION REQUIRED
Are you alive?
Hello?!?
you suck.

6

The Inbox of Shame

PRODUCTIVITY METHODS TREAT THE INBOX AS A
SPECIAL PLACE, BUT SOME OF US HAVE COME TO
VIEW OUR INBOX AS A SPECIAL PLACE IN HELL.

"Chris, are you there? We need to hear from you."

Thus began the third follow-up email from the events manager at a nonprofit. We'd been talking—several months earlier—about a big fundraiser they'd been planning. They wanted me to be part of an online summit they were hosting, or at least they had wanted me.

After an encouraging initial conversation, however, I'd dropped off the map. I didn't reply to the email asking for my bio and speaker details. I didn't open the message with a calendar link for our next check-in call. And despite the fact that I'd opened at least one of the follow-up emails (at least according to my email app when I looked later), I didn't respond to any of them.

It wasn't a situation about money. If I'd missed out on a corporate sponsorship for my podcast, for example, I'd still feel bad—but not this bad. There was no money involved in this deal; the nonprofit was run by a friend and for a cause I supported. Now I'd let down my friend, the organization, and of course, myself.

The next day, I told myself, I'd probably do the same thing all over again, in some other way.

This cycle wasn't my imagination. I really was dropping balls and letting people down. Moreover, this wasn't just during a busy season, like when I had a book due or big project in the works. It had simply grown to become my normal operating method.

I began almost every email with a version of the same sentence: "So sorry for the delay in reply. . . ."

Most of the time, people were gracious about this. "It's cool, things are crazy these days!" they'd reply, no matter the season or situation. But of course, *they'd reply,* which created another loop of communication, magnified many times by all the messages we'd exchange. I hadn't stemmed the tide; I'd only managed to tread water yet again.

And, yes, I also didn't like the fact that having all this communication with others felt like I was being invaded. For the most part, these were people I wanted to hear from, at least when I wasn't so overwhelmed. I wasn't worried about ignoring spam messages, sales pitches, or even some notes that didn't necessarily need a reply. But I'd already dealt with all of those—it was everything else that made me feel like I was drowning.

My colleagues and close friends grew accustomed to the fact that they might not hear back from me if they asked me a question. It was obvious to anyone who paid attention (and even to me, despite my lack of attention) that I was falling way behind. In fact, I appreciated the honesty of the few people who said outright that they were disappointed to not hear from me. I understood their perspective—I was disappointed, too!

• • •

One time I had a nightmare. In my dream, I had forgotten to respond to an email from a friend about a reimbursement from six months earlier. I woke up in a sweat, wondering if I really had neglected their messages all that time. I decided to wait until the morning to check, but knowing that I'd likely forget, I made a quick note on my phone.

The next morning I encountered another surprise. I managed to remember the dream without the digital reminder, which was good because it turned out I hadn't actually made the note. Instead, *in my dream* I had opened-up my task management app and added a note: "Check on reimbursement."

This whole process—the missing email, the reminder, the promise to myself to try harder—was hard-coded in me at this point.

I know how silly it might sound: *I had a nightmare about an email.* But the stress was real! The nightmare was a subconscious, cognitive distortion that reinforced my belief that I would never get better at communicating. The psychic distress I experienced in always feeling behind was real, too.

Time anxiety was a constant companion, even in the midst of joyous events. If I traveled to a place I enjoyed, if I did something fun—wherever I was and whatever I was doing, it was always looming in the background. The distress robbed me of feeling present. How could I catch up? I wondered, over and over. Once in a great while I managed to get current on most issues, but the rare feeling of "inbox zero" afterglow didn't last long.

When You're Drowning, You Can't Just Swim Faster

If you relate to any of this—perhaps with different details but a similar sense of guilt and anxiety underpinning your daily existence—you're not alone. As I conducted surveys and interviews on the topic of time anxiety, I learned that these feelings weren't uncommon at all. One reader wrote: "Sometimes I can't breathe. I get migraines. I wake up in the night and think about all the calls I forgot to return."

Someone who doesn't relate might think this is strange. Are people really that stressed out about missed messages? Well, time anxiety doesn't affect everyone that way, but yes, missed messages are a major problem for many of us. We have internalized the belief that availability, or even mere responsiveness, is synonymous with excellence.

So what's the answer to overcoming this distress? First, here's what it isn't. The answer is not just *get more organized*. From much experience and many attempts, I can tell you that organization on its own will not solve the problem. I'll give you some specific tips shortly, but it's important to understand that trying to be on top of everything, all the time, is a recipe for disaster.

• • •

Let's consider how the popular Getting Things Done (GTD) method would solve the problem. For all the things that bother you, it would first suggest that you "get them out of your head," as in, capture everything that's on your mind in written form. Then you go through the list of items and "process" them into tasks and supplemental material according to a set of rules.

Fair enough, but here's problem one with that approach: some of what's bothering you is in your head, but much more lies waiting in your inbox—or more likely, your inboxes, if you consider all the different digital platforms where messages can accumulate.

GTD treats the inbox as a special place, whereas many of us have come to view our inbox as a special place in hell. It's an untamable beast that will always want to be fed, even soon after it's eaten.

Problem two: If you do manage to "capture" every possible task that comes to mind, you now have yet another list. Don't you already have lists of some kind? Lists are neither the problem nor the solution. (They're just lists.)

Whatever process you choose, GTD and other productivity methods suggest you are capable of handling everything that comes your way, if only you'd improve your work habits. *Prepare for the deluge,* it encourages you. *Stand your ground.*

In short, the suggested remedy is to become superhuman. (Funny enough, a popular email app for tech-savvy users is called Superhuman. Not subtle!)

Consider the ultimate outcome of living life fully by the rules of this operating system. Under these conditions, the best possible scenario is that you will become a highly functional manager of someone else's dreams and goals. You are an inbox-processing ninja, charting your course through meeting reminders, requests for input, and newsletters you've unsubscribed to but still keep coming. At the end of the day, somehow you've managed to perform exactly as other people prefer.

I ALWAYS RETURNED SUSAN'S CALLS

Good job! Now you get to do it all over again tomorrow.

At the end of your life, you'll be able to look back with pride and say, "The meeting minutes were always filled out properly. I always returned Susan's calls. I showed up to videoconferences, many times."

This is not what life should be about.

Alternatively, you could do something else: admit your inability to become superhuman, freely acknowledge that your attempts to keep your communication up-to-date will always be futile—and get on with living, as best as you can and in the way you've always wanted to.

You can still have systems and tools. You just need to rethink your relationship with "mastering" your inbox.

Email Survival Tips

These tips can be applied to or modified for any types of recurring communication, including workplace platforms, group chats, or DMs:

- Use the "delayed send" feature when batching replies. This helps you avoid the trap of being hyper-responsive and also cuts down on a lot of back-and-forth emailing throughout the day.
- If you have email anxiety around opening and reading the messages (this happens to me a lot), understand that your feelings won't simply get better with the passing of time. It's usually better to face this head-on and spend a few minutes deciding on a next step—like a quick response acknowledging receipt, for example.

- Send shorter responses in favor of long replies. "Let's talk about this" is a great way to acknowledge a message without spending half an hour writing a response. (Do you then need to schedule a time to talk about the topic in question? Sometimes yes, sometimes no. It might just naturally come up later, saving you the need to actively manage it in advance.)

- Play the role of an email-responding actor. I got this idea from a commentor on Reddit, who shared this story in response to a student who was overwhelmed with their inbox:

  "I have come up with a solution. I think it will sound a little funny, but it works for me: **I pretend in my head that I'm acting and that I'm playing the part of the best email responder in the world.** So let's say you have an email to respond to. Don't worry, you don't have to answer the email, you just have to play the part of the person who answers the email. There's no need to worry about it, because in your head, you're playing a part, you're acting. I know it sounds a bit odd, but I promise you, it works."

Again, you're not going to be perfect at dealing with your inbox. The tips in the previous pages are designed to help you work smarter and faster, but you'll be even better off by removing the expectation that your inbox is something to master.

Responsiveness Is Not the Highest Value

Overcoming the burden of an overstuffed inbox is a lot like life itself: you can try "hacking" it all you want, but in the end, the outcome is the same for everyone. Much better to make your peace with it and get on with living.

Experiencing the cycle of inbox shame made me think differently about some people I'd tried to connect with at one point or another. When I started writing books, I reached out by email to authors of other books that had inspired me throughout the years. Most of them responded, usually with a short note in a decent amount of time. But some remained elusive, immune to follow-ups or even introductions through mutual friends.

I looked up to the authors who wrote me back personally, and I thought the others were standoffish. Now that I was struggling to reply to emails too, I realized that the ones who were purposefully more withdrawn might be on to something.

They weren't deliberately rude, they were just overwhelmed! The fact that my email or direct message didn't fall at the top of their priority list made sense.

• • •

So what did I do? I became one of the people who didn't pretend to be so responsive. Every January, I instituted a new "email bankruptcy" practice, where I simply archived everything I'd missed from the previous year. I'd done a version of this in the past, but then I'd send out a sheepish message to all my contacts explaining that if there was something they still needed, please send me another message.

Now I stopped doing that and simply archived. If I still needed access to something later, it was just a search away. In the meantime, I could move forward with less angst.

What's done is done, I figured—or in this case, what's undone is done.

At first it felt painful. I was giving up on lots of unanswered messages! But the pain was temporary, because once the inbox was empty, I was able to be much more responsive to newer messages—at least for a while.

I also updated my priority settings, so that I'd more quickly see messages from a small number of people. I learned to pay much more attention to this subset of messages than all the others.

Don't get me wrong, though: trying to make my inbox a well-oiled machine was the problem, not the solution. That's why even though those things helped somewhat, there was one more approach that made more of a difference than anything else.

The Power of Doing What You Can

After hiding from my inboxes day in and day out, I decided to turn them into a ritual. The ritual was to do what I can, for a certain amount of time, and not worry (as much) about the rest. Completion was no longer the goal. I wasn't going to hyper-optimize to the point of perfection, but I also didn't want to fully retreat.

Approaching your inbox is as simple as that. Just set a timer for twenty minutes and do what you can. Are you behind on a bunch of messages? Pick the most urgent and respond until the time's up. Do you need to draft notes for a presentation? Start writing!

It's like the Pomodoro Technique, except you track your progress not by what remains (the ocean never dries up!) but by what you're able to do.

That point bears restating: when the time is up, you celebrate what you've done, instead of dwelling on what remains. You can do another round later, or even right after taking a short break if you feel up to it. Just remember: you're not trying to win the war. You're just doing what you can to be as thorough as humanly possible—while still being human.

Where possible, prioritize these items:

- Anything that's urgent or extremely important*
- Something that truly helps someone, even in a small way
- Something that makes you feel good
- Something that's proactive, not just responsive

Combine this habit with paying active attention and notice how it feels to "get things done" in this manner—not with the goal of completion, but the practice of progress.

• • •

I would love to tell you that I eventually worked everything out with the guy who was emailing me from the nonprofit. In the rom-com version of a business story, it would conclude with an update about how it was good that I wasn't super responsive to

---

* Apply a high filter to labeling things as urgent or important. Most things in life are neither, but it's easy to get in the trap of letting other people define your priorities.

him at first, because it ended up . . . I don't know, somehow being better later?

But I promised you only true stories. Nothing really happened at all after that, except I felt bad, and I tried to try harder, and ultimately this effort led me to what I said about "doing what you can." That's all that's possible! So that's what I've tried to do in similar situations ever since, knowing full well that sometimes I'm going to get it wrong.

There's no shame in giving up the goal of always being available. As your life gets busier, you simply won't be able to respond to everything. You might feel superhuman from time to time, but this is deceptive. In the long run, this feeling will make you anxious about all that remains undone, and then you'll feel anxious about feeling anxious.

At the same time, be careful about abdicating your responsibilities entirely. That's another form of defeat, and it won't help with the shame you feel in being unresponsive. That's why the best way forward is to do what you can and let go of the rest. You're still here *now*. You can't do everything, but you can do *something*. Do that thing and hold your head high.

Hyper-responsiveness doesn't equal excellence, happiness, or even the best use of our limited time. We have to set our own limits, because no one else will.

PRACTICE

Set a "No-Guilt Rule" with a Friend

BUILD A STRONGER RELATIONSHIP WITH A
LIFELONG FRIEND BY MUTUALLY COMMITTING TO NOT
FEELING GUILT OVER LAPSING IN COMMUNICATION.
YOU CAN ALWAYS PICK IT BACK UP!

I bet you have at least one friend you talk to regularly but not all the time. You might communicate over text, voice note, email, or some other medium—but whatever it is, you keep a long-standing thread of open discussion.

Sometimes, when you owe the other person an update, you might start to feel anxious as time passes. The anxiety turns to guilt (or perhaps, the anxiety remains and the guilt arrives as well!) until you finally send a response, usually starting with a lengthy apology.

Here's a better way to handle this situation.

For years, my friend Gemma and I have texted and sent each other voice notes off and on. We don't talk every day, and sometimes we don't talk for weeks or months at a time. But then we catch up, and it's as if we didn't have the long gap.

I forget which one of us had the idea, but at some point we introduced a "no-guilt rule" for our communication. We both know the other person is busy. We've each fallen behind at different points in the back-and-forth. We know that falling behind isn't a sign that the relationship isn't important to us. Similarly, reconnecting is something that should be done out of the value you place on the relationship, not out of guilt. (To restate: connecting less when you're busy doesn't mean you no longer value the relationship, and choosing to reconnect after an absence is a sign of the value the relationship holds.)

Simply having no guilt—it helps to acknowledge this directly—can remove the negative feelings associated with an overwise positive relationship. Then, when you're able to be more communicative, you can skip the long apologies and get back to the good stuff.

Take a picture of this story and send it to that friend of yours. Maybe the no-guilt rule can help both of you in the future.

7

The Magical Thinking of Time Management

TIME MANAGEMENT IS A POWERFUL STORY
BUILT ON AN ENTIRELY FALSE PREMISE.

Okay, let's lighten up a little bit. A book about time anxiety should not make you feel more anxious than you already do!

The point is that thinking about hard things, even the difficulty of making exclusive choices, can help us be more purposeful. We can feel hope for the future and live better today. I'll come back to this more later. For now, consider something easier: Santa Claus. I presume you've heard of him?

Depending on where and how you were brought up, you may have been told about Santa from a young age. Most likely, at some stage of childhood, this Santa myth was then shattered. You learned that there wasn't a guy from the Arctic Circle who traveled around the world every December 24 to leave presents at the home of every child. (It makes for a great story, until you begin to think about the logistics.)

Believing in Santa is a relatively harmless myth for most kids. But there's another myth that many adults swear by, and this one is much more damaging. If you're reading this book, the odds are high that you've been indoctrinated into an invasive, mytho-logical story. This belief has consequences far greater than the belief in fairy tales.

The myth you have been told is that you can manage time.

. . .

You've heard of time management, right? Just kidding, of course you have. You hear about it every day. This fable is told in count-less ways, from bestselling books on productivity, to entire sub-cultures of videos on every social network.

There are more than sixty thousand books on Amazon that reference "time management." For the low fee of $75,000, your company can hire a keynote speaker who will pump up your employees and give them "tips" on managing their time.

Yet something is fundamentally wrong with the entire con-cept. Time exists independently of us and does not like to be told what to do. Time passes when you sleep, when you procras-tinate, when you worry about time running out, or when you're having the time of your life. In all these situations (and every other), time marches on.

Time is also the greatest nonrenewable resource in the world. If you run out of milk, you can go to the store. If you run out of money, you can find a way to get more of it. If you run out of time—you're done.

The misunderstanding of time management informs much of our modern way of life, especially in the Western world. You are encouraged to buy fancy planners, learn new methods or sys-tems, and generally create productive habits to be a better man-ager of a resource that is fiercely independent. You are rewarded at work for being an expert at an imaginary discipline. And so you dutifully attempt everything you can to maximize your time, to write better lists, to juggle more obligations, to become a better human or at least a more caffeinated one.

And yet—you end up being stressed out. You feel overwhelmed. There are things you aren't doing that you feel you should. There are things you're doing that you'd like to stop, but you don't know how.

At the end of the day, you wonder, "Where did the time go?"

Time management does not deal with time anxiety, the feeling of being crushed by the scarcity of time and the inevitability of things ending.

So here's a crazy idea. *What if all those things you do to try to stay ahead are holding you back? What if there's a much better way of interacting with time?*

The fault is not in you but in a collective delusion, one that pushes a narrative built on an entirely false premise. No matter how hard we push, we cannot manage time.

Accepting this fact is the first step to being free of the obligation to try.

Radical Acceptance

It might be hard to accept that there is no such thing as time management. After all, you've been deeply conditioned to believe in it. But just think about this: If you really could manage time, what would you do with this power? Would you really just use it to study harder, host more efficient meetings, or be a better girl boss?

A true time-management ninja would be more ambitious. If that was you, you'd do things like:

- Tell time that it needs to slow down ("Time, you're going too fast!")
- Tell time to pause while you sleep for as long as you want
- Tell time that once in a while, you're going to need a few extra hours in the day
- Create an instant delay of time's passing for as long as you need, especially when an important deadline is approaching
- "Bank" extra time for later, so you can pick and choose the flow of time to suit your needs
- Create an "eternal weekend" for that vacation that never ends

You get the idea. Are you able to do any of those things? If so, you're a superhero with a much more useful power than smashing through walls or becoming invisible. (Please share your secrets.)

Assuming that your powers over the whims of time are as nonexistent as everyone else's, this thought exercise should illustrate the point. However alluring it may seem, the idea of time management is a lie.

So then, since we can't manage time—what do we do? I promised you good news.

Here it is: there is a much, much better way to interact with time. It will allow you to feel immediate relief, as well as give you tools you can use for a brighter future.

It starts with a concept called *radical acceptance*. In its simplest phrasing, radical acceptance is a formula: **pain + resistance equals suffering**. It assumes that in every life, some amount of pain is unavoidable. Suffering, however, comes from trying to fight against this unavoidable pain.

This bears emphasizing:

PAIN:
NOT OPTIONAL, CAN'T SKIP IT,
HAPPENS TO EVERYONE

SUFFERING:
OPTIONAL, HAPPENS WHEN
YOU RESIST THE PAIN

Think of a time in your life in which you were hurt, and the hurt compounded (got worse) because of your resistance to it. It might have been a bad breakup, a job or promotion you didn't get, or any other number of things.

What can you control in those situations? You can't control the pain itself, which comes from an outside event. You can, however, choose not to resist—and thus not to suffer.*

• • •

One time I was applying for a prestigious scholarship in grad school. I'd put a lot of work into my application, pestering my professors for recommendation letters, writing what I thought was an intelligent application essay, and otherwise making sure my application was as strong as possible. Many people were ap-

---

* The concept of radical acceptance is based on the work of Marsha M. Linehan and Tara Brach. It offers a mindfulness approach to self-acceptance and healing from past traumas. Check out Tara Brach's book *Radical Acceptance* to learn more.

plying for this scholarship, but I had high hopes that I'd win it. Shockingly, the application committee made a different choice!

When I received the polite rejection email ("We had many great candidates," it assured me), I took the news poorly. The message didn't invite further communication, but within an hour I'd composed a reply. I thanked the committee but explained that I really needed the scholarship. Would it be possible to meet with some committee members in person, or perhaps have a phone call? That way, they could get to know me better.

I should have waited a day before sending that message (because then I wouldn't have sent it), but I didn't. To their credit, the kind person who responded to explain that the decision was final was nice. I guess my desperate email wasn't the first or only one they'd received in protest.

It's embarrassing to recall that incident now. I can still remember the sting of reading that rejection notice—but I also know that I made it worse by trying to protest.

It Still Hurts, But Now You Can Move Forward

To be clear, radical acceptance doesn't mean you're happy about the pain you experience. Pain hurts. Getting older, being rejected, constantly feeling behind and hesitant—these things aren't fun.

It also doesn't mean you must approve of or continue to be in a situation that's harmful, like a toxic relationship. You should get out of that relationship as soon as you can, and then you radically accept what lies in the past.

When it comes to time anxiety, radical acceptance means you stop resisting the passage of time. You stop trying to control the uncontrollable. You understand that time will pass with or without you. You make plans, but you hold them loosely. If an unexpected event derails your schedule, you adjust your timeline without self-judgment. You fully expect that your energy and output will vary day by day due to factors beyond your control.

Paradoxically, when you give up the fight, you gain something more valuable: the chance to make a difference in something you can influence.

Recognizing that there are real limits to your abilities should feel refreshing. Your defeat in the war against time opens up all sorts of other possibilities. By losing this war, you gain the ability to be much happier (and also more effective) in the rest of your life.

Benefits of radical acceptance include:

- Energy conservation: radical acceptance frees up mental and emotional energy previously spent fighting against time, allowing you to redirect it toward something more meaningful.
- Present-moment focus: by accepting the passage of time, you can better engage with the present, enhancing your quality of life and relationships.
- Improved decision-making: with a clearer mind, unburdened by the compulsion to control, you can make more thoughtful choices about how to spend your time.

Once you choose to reject the myth of time management . . . look out! Now you're ready to unlock some real superpowers.

As with embracing the facts of your mortality, now you can see what everyone else has been avoiding. This knowledge gives you freedom! It can nudge you toward brave choices and bold decisions, and you will be free from the burden of accounting for every minute of your time.

You don't have to be a getting-things-done superhero, because no one else really is. The difference between you and others who try is that you've chosen to stop fighting this truth and move on to better things.

• • •

Just like children believe in myths to make sense of the world they're growing up in, adults hold on to the idea of time management as a way to make sense of their chaotic lives. Both are shortcuts to understanding more complicated truths—and while one belief is harmless, the other can be harmful.

Thankfully, everything gets much easier when you stop trying to do the impossible.

Stop believing you can boss time around. Instead, accept the relief of giving up control. Life is short, and your time is valuable—but respecting the limits of both can be liberating.

PRACTICE

The Reverse Bucket List

MAKE A LIST OF THE AMAZING THINGS
YOU'VE ALREADY DONE.

In the pursuit of future goals, we often overlook the milestones we've already achieved. So instead of skipping over all of your past accomplishments, consider making a list of them. It's like making a bucket list, just, well, in reverse.

Start your list with the obvious things that come to mind—in whatever categories you think of—but don't stop there. A good bucket list (as in, one that contains goals for the future) usually features items from a range of different categories: personal, professional, "adventure-y," and so on.

Do the same for your retrospective list: diversify the categories so you can reflect on many different things you've already accomplished. Be proud of yourself!

Finally, the reverse bucket list can be more than just a trip down memory lane. It might inspire you to set some new goals or to revisit previous accomplishments and tackle them again in a new way.

Here are some examples of reverse bucket list items from other readers, just in case they might be helpful in bringing something to your mind:

- Performed on stage in a community play
- Saved up for a down payment on a home

- Read fifty books in a year
- Ran a half-marathon
- Went on a solo international trip
- Negotiated a raise with my company
- Adopted a pet
- Hiked every major trail in Utah
- Learned a new language
- Gave a presentation to a large audience

• • •

Personal note: As someone who tends to be future-minded, I often struggle with recognizing what I've already done. This exercise was especially helpful to me, as a number of accomplishments came to mind that I'd totally forgotten until I focused on them.

8

What Is Enough?

DECIDE ON A LOGICAL FINISH LINE FOR
PROJECTS AND DAILY WORK.

Jessica's day was full of meetings and deadlines. She liked her work as a freelance writer, but there was one big problem: the work never ended. Once one assignment was complete, she simply moved on to another.

Even if she cleared her to-do list for the day, many of the completed tasks morphed into follow-up items. The task "Brainstorm ideas for new story pitches" turned into "Send pitches to editors." "Finish first draft" became "Review and edit first draft."

There was always one more thing to do.

Even if you're not self-employed, you might recognize some parts of Jessica's situation. When there are no real constraints on working more, many of us have become conditioned to the idea that *work simply never ends*. This becomes exhausting and all-consuming—even when we otherwise enjoy the work itself. The lack of milestones and end points prevents us from developing a sense of accomplishment, which is helpful in feeling purposeful.

Though it's not always easy to enforce, the problem also points to an obvious solution: *decide for yourself what is enough work for any particular day.*

Many of Us Treat Work as a Never-ending Cycle

Like Jessica, many people work at jobs or in careers that have an unlimited number of things to do. Working this way is like playing a tower-defense game, where a horde of enemies approaches your castle. You can usually defeat them at first, but they get stronger—and they keep coming. Whenever you deal with one attacking horde of tasks, it just means you've leveled up in order to face a new invasion.

It's very easy to fall into this pattern. Lots of people live their whole lives this way. They do so even if the loop only serves to increase their sense of anxiety while further advancing someone else's interest, typically that of their employer.

In the corporate world, some workers have solved this problem by "quiet quitting," where they purposely limit the amount of work they do. In the world of manufacturing, this tactic is called a slowdown. Employees are working, but they're not working particularly hard, and no one is going "above and beyond."

To be clear, I don't think quiet quitting is an ideal solution for most people. If your job sucks, you might as well *just quit*, either quietly or otherwise. But the idea of applying self-designed limitations is helpful.

How to Decide What Is Enough

My situation is a lot like Jessica's, in the sense that I work for myself and often have multiple projects in different stages of completion. I love working on my own, but when the work never ends, I tend to get overwhelmed and anxious. Instead of feeling proud of what I'd been able to do in one day, I always focused on what was undone.

There's an obvious solution here: if milestones and end points don't exist, make them. Ask yourself:

1. What is enough for today?
2. What is enough for this project?
3. What is enough to fulfill the commitment I make to my job?

Once you reach "enough," pause before continuing. Instead of tackling yet another task in zombie mode, check in with yourself using the tools and intuitive model you've been learning. What do you need right now? What is the best choice at this moment?

What Does Done Look Like?

Decide on a logical "finish line" for projects and daily work.

If you work for yourself, or even if you work on your own for large parts of the day, the question of "What does done look like?" can be especially difficult to answer. In our modern world, there's always something else to start or advance.

That's why it can be helpful to decide what "done" looks like whenever you're starting something new. This could be completing a big project or just the day's work. When you set a finish line, you give yourself something to look forward to. Then, upon completion, you have something to celebrate, or at least take satisfaction in.

Adopting this approach doesn't mean you stop striving or

challenging yourself. There might also be times where you're so excited about something that you lose track of the hours and just keep going—a practice that can be fun and useful in some circumstances.

Deciding what "done" means helps you avoid the trap of facing infinite work without any concept of completion.

· · ·

Aside from those times when I avoided a dreaded task, my problem wasn't starting the work; my problem was stopping. Some people struggle with getting started, but I'm usually able to hack that by using Pomodoro timers, where I commit to work on something for a certain amount of time (typically twenty to thirty minutes) before taking a short break. The best part about the Pomodoro Technique, properly applied, isn't that it puts you to work but that it limits your work. The break between sessions is a key feature.

Applying the concept further, I began to set goalposts for my workday. Not endless to-do lists, but a couple of important priorities. The word *priorities* is helpful in this scenario: it suggests a very limited number of items. In contrast, if everything's important, nothing is.

Because I was often unhappy with myself, I also tried to improve my ability to take pride in how I spent my time. Most days weren't perfect, but did I spend less than an hour on mindless internet surfing? If so, great! A few other questions proved helpful:

1. Did I create something?
2. Did I help someone?
3. Did I take some amount of time for myself?

The act of answering these questions morphed into a quick checklist that I sometimes referred to when walking in my nearby park before sunset. I always carry a notebook with me, so I'd stop and jot down what I did that was aligned with the priorities I identified.

That was it. No affirmations, no scientific review, no detailed procedural to plan the next day. I just asked myself what would be enough, and when the feelings of overwhelm crept in later, I tried to remember the answers.

When work is potentially endless, decide for yourself what the end points will be. You can always add something to these end points later if you want, but the sense of completion and accomplishment will help you feel better.

PRACTICE

Free Time in the Middle of the Day

DON'T SAVE ALL YOUR "FUN" TIME FOR EVENINGS
AND WEEKENDS.

If you work somewhat regular hours, you've likely settled into a routine that involves long stretches of work on most weekdays. When you think about free time, your mind naturally goes to evenings and weekends.

To begin placing a higher value on leisure, try to reclaim some of your working time *for yourself*.

Start with small steps, like taking an hour off in the afternoon. Go for a walk, take a yoga class, visit an art show, or do anything out of the ordinary during your normal workday. Graduate to seeing a movie—at the theater, if possible. Sitting in a theater in the afternoon feels different than sitting in front of a screen at home, where you may already be used to spending time in some form for your job.

Then, assuming you have the option, start reclaiming more of your time this way each week. This won't be possible for everyone, I realize. But if it's possible in some way for you, try it out and see how it feels.

9

Do Things Poorly

OVERWRITE THE IDEA THAT EVERYTHING YOU
DO MUST BE EXCELLENT. MANY THINGS ARE
PERFECTLY FINE IF THEY'RE "GOOD ENOUGH."

Whether you had a Santa phase as a child or not, you might have grown up internalizing another belief. This one is more complex than a belief in Santa, and just like the myth of time management, it's a belief that can be limiting.

It's the idea that you should *always do your best work.*

Let's challenge that belief. For a number of reasons, sometimes it's better to do significantly less than your best work. Instead of pursuing perfection, or even "excellence," your life can be much better if you instead *do things poorly.*

I know this may sound counterintuitive, especially if you grew up feeling pressured to always get good grades and finish at the head of the pack in competitive activities.

I first learned of this concept from a viral thread by Heron Greenesmith,[*] a policy attorney and advocate for LGBTQ issues. Here's how they put it:

---

[*] In addition to Heron Greenesmith, I'm grateful to Gabrielle Blair (@designmom) for bringing the "do things poorly" concept to my attention.

F*ck perfection. Art? Do it poorly. School work? Do half rather than not doing it at all. Calling a friend? Text them if you're afraid to call rather than not talking to them at all.

Parenting? Literally just be there, even if you're half-asleep and on your phone. Eating? Go to McDonald's rather than waiting for something perfect.

Again, I realize this advice might seem contrary to what you're used to hearing. Maybe it's even contrary to what you tell yourself. You want to do a good job at everything! But this desire for all-around excellence could be stressing you out.

Being a perfectionist is not something to be proud of—it's based on a belief system that can limit all kinds of important skills, including:

- Your ability to complete simple tasks and move on
- Your ability to feel a sense of accomplishment about anything
- Your ability to triage, noting the difference between the few things that are truly important and everything else

These potential limitations are why it's helpful to remember that not everything—or maybe even most things—needs to be done with excellence.

Heron makes the point that doing things poorly isn't just about being able to move faster in the world. In fact, there's a much more important reason, which they explained later in the thread: "Doing things poorly is CRUCIAL to harm reduction."

If you're trying to stop using harmful substances, for example, maybe you'd benefit from simply using less of them. This might be easier than never using, which is difficult for some people who struggle with addiction. The story of "needing to quit" and being unable to can be harmful.

It's Not Just Recycling or Eating at McDonald's

I like the example Heron gives of eating at McDonald's if you're hungry and can't easily identify a better option. Many of us might intuitively reject this suggestion. "I would never!" I can hear some people saying. "Fast food is bad."

But you know what's better than not eating? Eating. And maybe the next time you order groceries or stop at the store, you'll remember to get some healthy snacks so you'll have alternatives. For now, you eat the Big Mac, because eating is good.

Another example of doing things poorly comes from KC Davis, a counselor and author who advises people to just throw things away when cleaning up their living spaces, instead of always feeling the pressure to recycle or feeling responsible for finding new homes for every unwanted thing.

Don't miss the point: recycling is good, and you probably shouldn't eat at McDonald's all the time. But when you're feeling overwhelmed, taking action is better than not taking action. It can help you move into a better place, so that you're then able to make different choices next time.

Think about how else you could apply the "do things poorly" method:

PROBLEM: You struggle to complete classwork.

SOLUTION: Lower your standards. Turn in work that is less than amazing, and use the extra time to do something else. You don't need perfect grades in every class.

• • •

PROBLEM: Your living space feels messy, but you're exhausted.

SOLUTION: Identify what REALLY needs to be cleaned up. Do as much as you can (for those things only) for ten minutes. Once the time is up, stop cleaning and move on.

• • •

PROBLEM: You're burdened with a huge pile of unread messages.

SOLUTION: DELETE all unread messages and start over. Instead of flailing about and trying to catch up, just try to do a better job with new messages going forward, at least for a while.

• • •

PROBLEM: You haven't returned a phone call.

SOLUTION: It happens. Don't worry about it. You can always resume the conversation later if it's important.

If you think of yourself as a perfectionist, I know this concept of doing things poorly is difficult—maybe even terrifying! But think about what you could accomplish if you did some things poorly. Not only will you live to tell the tale, you'll have more energy to spend on something else. Read the next section for an example.

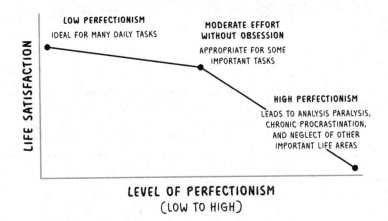

LIFE SATISFACTION / LEVEL OF PERFECTIONISM (LOW TO HIGH)

LOW PERFECTIONISM
IDEAL FOR MANY DAILY TASKS

MODERATE EFFORT WITHOUT OBSESSION
APPROPRIATE FOR SOME IMPORTANT TASKS

HIGH PERFECTIONISM
LEADS TO ANALYSIS PARALYSIS, CHRONIC PROCRASTINATION, AND NEGLECT OF OTHER IMPORTANT LIFE AREAS

Don't Half-Ass It— Three-Quarters-Ass Is Good Enough

Thinking about doing things poorly brought to mind a story from my experience. You might know the expression "half-ass," which is usually used as an admonition, that is, "Don't half-ass it." Give it all you've got, in other words.

On the events team I used to lead, we had a saying about this mentality. With a big conference coming up and many different moving parts to plan for, we wanted the core experience to be excellent. But if we tried to pursue excellence everywhere, inevitably we'd fall short. So we made a rule that whenever we found ourselves getting bogged down in some tiny detail that probably wouldn't matter much, anyone on the team could speak up in favor of what we called the *three-quarters-ass rule.*

In essence, the rule was: sure, we don't want to half-ass anything. Let's try to do a good job. But not everything requires a full level of engagement. So instead, let's figure out the minimally acceptable solution for whatever we're stuck on, then move on to bigger things.

Feel free to adopt or modify this strategy however it suits you. Just remember: not everything can be done with excellence, so you'll feel much less anxious if you stop trying to meet an impossible standard.

Doing things poorly might also allow you to focus on the few things that really matter, perhaps doing an even better job with those. When in doubt, let go and move on.

PRACTICE

Choose What to Keep Up With

KEEPING UP WITH EVERYTHING IS IMPOSSIBLE,
SO STOP TRYING TO.

"It's so hard to keep up these days!"

You may have heard someone say that, or you may have said it yourself. But guess what? It's not just hard to keep up, it's impossible.

There's a twenty-four-hour news cycle, another cycle about the cycle itself, and endless loops that play off the ongoing cycles. Meanwhile you have incoming messages in different mediums from all over the place.

This is part of what makes you anxious.

If you've already put a brick in an inbox or two, that's a good start. Next, try getting more intentional about what you choose to keep up with. You don't need to know about everything, and since you won't be able to do so anyway, choose and focus on a few specific areas.

If you're wondering how to limit the areas, there's an easy starting point. Begin with reducing, cutting, stripping away.

Unsubscribe, unfollow.

Condense and clear your to-do list.

Close those browser tabs you've been keeping open for three weeks. If you still need them later, you can always get them back.

A Short Summary of Part 1

It's hard to make rational decisions when you feel overwhelmed. Free up extra time however you can—perhaps by removing items from your calendar—so that you can begin to think more about the bigger picture.

"Time blindness" hinders your sense of time. An easy fix is to allow more time than you think you need. Leave ten to fifteen minutes earlier for every appointment, and resist the temptation to cram in one more thing.

"Time rules" are neurological patterns you've learned at some point, often subconsciously. Some can be helpful, but others that no longer serve you well should be discarded.

Instead of doing it all, practice the art of doing what you can. Devote small blocks of time to communication triage, where you try to clear as many high-value messages as possible, without getting further overwhelmed.

Radical acceptance is a concept that suggests some pain in life is inevitable, but much suffering can be limited when we stop resisting the pain.

Decide for yourself *what is enough*. Stop comparing yourself to someone else's situation. Set benchmarks for daily work, and then stop when you hit them.

Not everything needs to be done with excellence. You can conserve energy and accomplish more by accepting that sometimes it's okay to do things poorly.

INTERLUDE

The Gift and Burden of Choice

During a hard time in my life, I read a passage about a fig tree in a book by Sylvia Plath. In the book, the narrator sits under a tree that contains a number of juicy, delicious figs. Each fig represents a life choice: to be an Olympic athlete, to be a brilliant professor, and so on. Overwhelmed, the narrator is unable to choose from such a bounty of options, and one by one the ruined figs fall to the ground.

As I read the passage, I felt a deep sense of sadness. I too could see an abundance of options that awaited my selection—but many of them were exclusive, meaning that if I accepted one I'd have to turn down many others.

How could I possibly choose? What should I have been doing *right then*? I wanted more time to decide, but time didn't wait around for me. It operated on its own, without concern for my preferences.

I thought about the fig-tree analogy over and over. Like the book's narrator, I felt overwhelmed by the idea of deciding. For a long time, I remained stuck, unable to choose between competing directions—and, of course, not making a choice was also making a choice.

Looking back years later, I have a better understanding of this time in my life. Some of it was because I was clinically depressed, mildly at first and then more moderately. I ended up getting help through therapy and medication, and I'm grateful for both.

But the wistfulness I felt when considering Sylvia Plath's fig tree wasn't all born from a depressive season. Some of it stemmed from the state of being that can crop up in all parts of life, regardless of any situational factors or medical diagnosis.

What I was feeling when I read the description was time anxiety: not a clinical condition but a deeply felt, unnamed sense of frustration. I could improve my mood and still feel apprehensive about the future or worry that I wasn't working on the right things at any given moment. I could address chemical imbalances, learn about attachment theory, and get away from situations that were causing me harm—all good choices!—and still lack a concrete model for overcoming the sense of frustration.

Eventually I discovered it was my relationship with time itself that was the problem. I was trying to manage something that couldn't be managed. I continued to dwell on the simple truth illustrated so well by the figs on the tree: **time is limited, but desire is limitless.** These facts will always be in conflict. Simply put, there was more that I wanted to do than I'd ever be able to do.

Facing this simple truth was the first step to making peace with my inability to do everything.

PART 2

Rewriting Time Rules

You have the power to understand and
address the neurological and behavioral
factors behind time anxiety. Visualize
unlearning unhelpful beliefs and rewriting
the self-imposed rules that limit your time.
This section explores evidence-based
approaches for developing a healthier
relationship with time.

One man's glass
is half full.

The other man's glass
is half empty.

The right man drinks.

—TOM WAITS

10

Our Perception of Time Changes as We Age

HOW WE RESPOND TO TIME ANXIETY IS CONNECTED TO OUR PERCEPTION OF TIME'S PASSING. WHEN WE PERCEIVE A "TIME SHORTAGE," WE BECOME UNSETTLED.

Time anxiety is composed of two parts: time and anxiety. It's easy to see how the second part is a complex condition. Anxiety can be situational, or it can be generalized. It can be seasonal, occurring either during a particular time of year or a specific time in your life.

Compared to anxiety, time seems like a simple concept. But is it? It might surprise you to know that time is not an absolute. In the scientific community, debates about time abound. Physicists and astronomers argue over everything from the precise definition of time to whether there should be a universal concept of time at all. Most of us accept that a common understanding of time allows people to coordinate with one other, but that's a benefit, not a definition.

It's as though we all acknowledged the presence of rain falling from the sky ("because it makes the grass grow") but without any idea of where it came from.

No one in the science world is debating where the rain comes from. We know that the sun shines on the sea, vaporizing water into the sky. Water vapor turns into droplets, which collide with one another, forming clouds. When there are enough droplets, they fall from the clouds, eventually returning to the sea and completing the cycle.

Time, however, is much harder to pin down.

Time Passes Differently at Different Stages of Life

If the discussion of time's complexities seems abstract, consider how you think about time. If you're like most people, the way you perceive time changes as you age. At different ages you experience the same amount of time in different ways.

When you're young, time passes slowly. Your parents are *so old*. You simply can't fathom ever being the same age as most adults in your life.

From one birthday to the next, a great deal of change occurs. You count the days to important milestones like graduation or getting your driver's license. The waiting is *hard*. It seems like you won't ever grow up and become an adult.

But then of course, you do. And at some point, the years start passing more quickly. Time is going by so fast! You look back and think, "Where did the time go?" It's no longer impossible to imagine the age your parents or grandparents were when you were a child. In fact, you find the onset of "old age" (whatever you define it as) to be rapidly approaching. What felt maddeningly slow as a child becomes distressingly fast later in life.

Even as an adult, you can probably notice that time seems to pass differently depending on how you're spending it. At work, long meetings and dreaded tasks seem to take forever—but if you're fortunate to get in a flow state for some of the day, the time goes by much quicker.

Even though time is still the same as it's always been, objectively speaking, our perception of it changes as we age, as well as during different activities of normal life.

Why does this matter? Because a primary reason we experience time anxiety is connected to our perception of time's passing. When we perceive a "time shortage," we become unsettled. *Time is running out*, we think. Well, of course it is—but no more or less than it always has. It's only our perception of it that changes.

• • •

One common cause of time shortages is when we try to pack too much into a short amount of time, like a single day. When we do this, we inevitably encounter the reality that our plans were too ambitious, and then we feel unsettled. A *time crunch* sets in. Now we have to make rapid-fire changes to our plans, accepting compromises and trade-offs.

Some of that process may be normal and unavoidable, at least at certain points in our life, but many of us speed through the days with a time crunch as the constant state. It's the rule, not the exception.

This state of being is highly stressful. I would say that it's unsustainable, but because we are remarkably resilient beings, we're able to endure high levels of stress. *It's just not good for us.* And therefore we feel anxious.

The compromises we make along the way often come in the form of self-sacrifice. Because we are unable to do all that we would like, we are forced to deny ourselves some degree of pleasure, satisfaction, or sense of completion. Again, this produces discomfort.

The discomfort can occur in either of the two versions of time anxiety:

EXISTENTIAL:
TIME IS RUNNING OUT <u>IN MY LIFE</u>.

DAILY ROUTINE:
THERE'S NOT ENOUGH TIME <u>IN THE DAY</u>.

These problems are interconnected, though at different times you might feel a stronger sense of one than the other. The solutions are also interconnected: we need to do a better job with our days, so that we can take better care of our lives.

This might be a good place to start getting more practical. What's something you can do in your daily life that will help you feel more purposeful?

Similarly, have you thought about the big picture of life recently? It might be helpful to consider any long-term goals, dreams, or aspirations.

When we feel rushed, it's hard to function well in the moment. It's also difficult to plan for a different future. In the next chapter, you'll learn to create rules of engagement to help you proactively anticipate common interruptions. After that, you'll learn why facing hard situations head-on (instead of avoiding them) is another helpful strategy.

How we plan our days is how we live our lives. As you build a plan to respond to time anxiety, you'll gradually begin melding these two perspectives—individual days and our overall lives— together.

PRACTICE

Create a "Time-Free" Zone

SET ASIDE A DEDICATED HOUR TO ENGAGE IN JOYFUL
ACTIVITIES WITHOUT WORRYING ABOUT TIME.

In a world where time often feels like our most precious and limited resource, creating a "time-free" zone can be liberating. This activity will help you carve out a space in your life to temporarily free yourself from the pressures of the clock and focus on something you enjoy.

1. Set an Intention

Set your intention to create your time-free zone by choosing a specific day and time within the next week. Decide on a period where you can be undisturbed for at least one hour. Write down your intention: "I will create a time-free zone on [date] at [time] to focus on activities that bring me joy and fulfillment."

Put it on your calendar so that nothing else gets scheduled during this time.

2. Select Two or Three Activities

Think about activities that make you lose track of time and bring you joy. These could be hobbies, creative projects, spending time in nature, reading, or anything that makes you feel deeply engaged and happy. List these activities, aiming for two or three options that you can switch between if needed.

3. Find a Space

Find a comfortable, quiet place where you can create your time-free zone. This could be a cozy corner of your home (away from any work area), a quiet park, or any place where you feel relaxed and undisturbed. Gather any materials you need for your chosen activities.

4. Enter and Engage

When the time comes, go to your prepared space and begin your time-free zone. If it helps, set a timer for the duration you've chosen (at least one hour) to ensure you don't worry about the clock. Alternatively, you can simply decide to stop when you feel ready. Engage fully in your chosen activities without worrying about productivity or deadlines. Allow yourself to be fully present in the moment.

If your mind starts to drift to time-related concerns, gently bring your focus back to the activity at hand, reminding yourself that this is your time-free zone.

5. Reflect

After your session, take a few moments to reflect on your experience. Write down what activities you engaged in, how it felt to focus on these activities without the pressure of time, and any changes you noticed in your mood or mindset. Based on your reflection, decide when you will create your next time-free zone.

Aim to make this a regular practice, whether it's daily, weekly, or whenever you need a break. By doing so, you'll continually reap the benefits of living in the moment, free from the constraints of time.

11

Use Rules of Engagement to Decide Between Competing Requests

SET UP DEFAULT DECISIONS THAT HELP YOU
NAVIGATE THE CONFLICTS AND BUSYNESS OF LIFE.

When we perceive a time shortage, it's even more challenging to decide between competing demands on our time.

How do you spend your time each day? What should you be doing right now? After you finish that task, what should you do next? And how will you respond to schedule conflicts, too many things on your plate, and competing requests for your time?

As you're well aware, there is a seemingly unlimited number of ways you could spend your time. Not only that, but throughout your day (and your week, your year, your life) you'll encounter all kinds of people who have their own ideas about what you should do.

To contain the overwhelm, I encourage you to use a concept called **rules of engagement, or ROEs**. These are guideposts that help you navigate decisions in the thick of the action. The concept comes from military practice, where battlefield commanders have to make quick, life-or-death decisions.

For example, commanders are supposed to respond with proportionality when their troops are attacked. If a unit is under fire by a sniper holed up in a village, they can't drop a thousand-pound bomb on the whole village to eliminate the threat. They're supposed to find a way to respond discriminately, targeting only the sniper and any other combatants in the area.

These rules also govern how prisoners of war are treated, the specific types of weapons that can be used (and what approvals are needed for each type), and many other stressful situations that come up in armed conflict.

We don't need to extend the military metaphor too much—you already know that life can feel like a battlefield, especially for busy people with a lot of responsibility. The point is this: ROEs can help you handle all the requests and opportunities that come your way.

To get started, think about where you tend to get sidetracked, derailed, or ambushed with something that throws you off course. These questions might help:

- What are the most common interruptions in your day?
- When do you feel most drained during your day or week?
- How often do you feel the need to escape your work environment?
- Do you find yourself needing time to recharge after social interactions or especially difficult tasks?
- Do you sometimes feel guilty or conflicted about putting work ahead of your health, yourself, or your family?
- What routines or activities do you most often sacrifice for work or other obligations?

Some interruptions truly are urgent and can't be prevented, but many others can be. Establish a rule that governs how you'll respond to some of the unnecessary interruptions.

A very simple starting point would be to turn off all the notifications on your phone for a set time every day. During this time, you decide to be unreachable except in the event of a true emergency. (With most phones, you can usually set up exceptions to the no-notification rule, like a call from your child's school.)

If you like to eat dinner with your family most nights, you can make a rule that this activity always trumps any other invitations. Or if you're not part of a dinner-eating family, maybe your rule is that you take a walk every evening where you listen to podcasts and relax from the day. Whenever something else presents itself during that window, you know what to do (turn it down) and don't need to waver.

Example Rules of Engagement for Inspiration

I've been surveying people to see how they use ROEs in the real world. In the next few pages, you can see some of their examples. Consider adopting or modifying any of them for yourself, or just see if any of them give you other ideas.

Setting a boundary for creative work:

Whenever possible, **I schedule meetings for after lunch instead of the morning.** Once in a while I have to meet earlier because of time zone issues or scheduling conflicts, but my default mode is to keep as much of my morning free as possible.

Limiting clients as a freelancer:

As a freelancer, I work with a set number of clients at one time. If someone wants to hire me when I'm fully booked, I offer to put them on a waiting list. **I learned the hard way that overcommitting myself doesn't help anyone.** As an added benefit, having a waiting list gets clients to take me more seriously. I've also been able to charge a higher rate for new clients, because they know that I'm in demand.

Prioritizing after-school pickups:

I work remotely and am responsible for picking up my son from school in the afternoon. **I'm a hard worker, but my boss and colleagues know that I'm simply not available in the 3:00 p.m. to 4:00 p.m. hour.**

One time I tried joining a conference call while I was in the carpool line, but the call went long and I wasn't able to pay attention to my son the whole ride back. After that, I decided that this time is sacred. It takes us twenty minutes to get home, and then we have a snack and play in the backyard for a few minutes before I resume work for another hour.

Calming nerves before public speaking:

I have to give presentations as part of my job. When I started, this was terrifying, but now it's merely nerve-wracking. I sometimes over-prepare and end up being jittery and frantic, even though I know the material. **Something I've learned is that before any meeting where I might need** to speak, I completely block out at least fifteen minutes in which I do nothing. I use this time to meditate and just be with myself. This fifteen-minute calming session is often just as good as an extra hour of preparation.

Cleaning the house without overcleaning the house:

I feel better when my apartment is clean, so I have a ritual of doing a deep-ish clean on Sunday afternoons. However, I sometimes also get stuck cleaning forever, and then I end the weekend feeling cranky and tired. **My new Rule of Engagement is to set a timer for ninety minutes. When it stops, I stop too—no matter what else "needs" to get done for it to feel spotless.** I've found that I can get a lot done in that time, and anything else is just being picky. I also prioritize better knowing that there's a countdown happening.

Training for a marathon:

Last year I ran my first marathon. It went well overall, but I didn't train for it as much as I would have liked. I'm now signed up for my second, and this time I created the whole twelve-week training schedule in advance. **To make sure I get it done, I made a rule that I don't allow myself to watch my nightly shows until I finish each day's workout.**

Most of the time this isn't a problem since I usually run in the morning, but sometimes I'm not able to get to it until after work. In those cases, I'm tempted to head to the couch and watch TV. But because of the rule, I head out the door to run first. Not going to lie, sometimes I don't want to do it. In the end I'm usually happy that I did, though. It's a case of a small sacrifice for long-term results.

As the last example of marathon training shows, ROEs can help you prioritize your own goals as well as maintain boundaries with others. If you have a week of exams that you need to be fresh for, you might decide in advance that you'll do whatever you need to in order to get to bed early those days. Then, if your friend asks you to go out late one night, you won't need to over-analyze the decision. "Not tonight," you can tell them. "Let's try again another time."

Another common self-imposed ROE is choosing to not look at your phone for an hour before bedtime, an hour after waking up, or both. Some people find that the before-bed rule helps them sleep better, and the morning rule helps them prepare for the day without getting immediately distracted by incoming news.

Whether your ROEs are designed to ward against outside distractions or help you maintain self-discipline (or both), they allow you to do more of what matters to you. They keep you aligned with your life purpose, and they give you the answer to the questions you've been struggling with. These questions might include:

- Everything seems important, but what is most important?
- How do I decide between competing interests, especially when I like multiple options?
- How can I feel more confident in my decisions, therefore reducing analysis paralysis and second-guessing myself less?
- What should I do *right now*?

By setting rules of engagement in advance, you'll have a built-in framework for responding to many choices that come up throughout your day. The rules can be as flexible as you need them to be, and you shouldn't hesitate to update them however you need.

PRACTICE

Learn to Ask, "Can This Wait?"

FOR MOST OF US, ONLY A FEW THINGS EVERY DAY ARE TRULY URGENT. LEARN TO SEPARATE REAL DEADLINES FROM IMAGINARY ONES.

Consider these questions:

1. What are some things in my life I feel unnecessarily pressured by?
2. How can I let go of these things, in order to thrive elsewhere?
3. Do other people try to rush or pressure me to move faster?

Most of the things we do in life can be done at many different times. You could do them right away, plan to do them later, or simply put them off for a while—sometimes a very long time. You wouldn't know this by how many people operate, though. They act as if every task and every request has the same level of "as soon as possible" urgency.

Living this way is stressful. It's simply not possible to operate at the same rate of speed all the time. Also, if everything is urgent, nothing is.

Therefore, as you take on different tasks throughout the day, learn to ask yourself: *What will happen if I don't complete this task right now? Is there a true consequence, or is the urgency self-imposed?*

Recognizing the difference can help you discern between what truly needs your immediate attention and what can be scheduled or postponed.

EXAMPLES OF THINGS THAT *CAN* WAIT:

1. Organizing your email inbox
2. Scheduling a nonurgent doctor's appointment
3. Cleaning out the garage or a closet
4. Responding to ordinary work emails
5. Preparing for a meeting that's days or weeks away
6. Updating a project with a distant due date
7. Helping a colleague with a task that isn't time-sensitive

EXAMPLES OF THINGS THAT *CAN'T* WAIT:

1. Picking up your child from school
2. Paying a bill that's due today
3. Attending a scheduled medical appointment
4. Completing a task with a fast-approaching deadline
5. Handling an emergency situation at work or home

When you feel overwhelmed by tasks, take a moment to write down everything you think needs to be done. As you review your list, pause and ask yourself, "Can this wait?" For each task, consider whether there will be significant consequences if it is delayed. Often, you'll find that many tasks don't need to be completed immediately and that the urgency you feel is self-imposed.

By identifying tasks that can wait, you remove the sense that everything is urgent. This allows you to make clearer decisions about what you really want to do.

Free yourself from imaginary deadlines. Learn to resist the siren call of false urgency.

Fear is a manipulative emotion that can trick us into living a boring life.

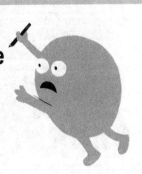

—DONALD MILLER

12

Be Right Back, I'm Just Going to Disappear and Never Return

AVOIDING HARD THINGS IS AN EVOLUTIONARY
DEFENSE MECHANISM. IT CAN FEEL GOOD
TEMPORARILY, BUT IT COMES WITH A LINGERING
PSYCHOLOGICAL COST.

A British man named Alan Knight facing charges of fraud came up with an unusual defense: he couldn't appear in court because he was in a coma. This wasn't a real coma, however. It was an act of desperation. Enlisting his wife's help—who later went to prison for her role in the affair—he managed to keep up the charade for more than two years.

To avoid trial, Knight even checked into a hospital for a ten-week stay. Medical tests showed that nothing was wrong with him, but his performance was so persuasive that some doctors concluded that he must have had some kind of mystery illness. Alas, the scheme unraveled after his discharge to home care, when CCTV captured images of Knight out on the town, doing some low-key grocery shopping and definitely not in a coma.

Over in the United States, a woman named Jennifer Wilbanks was facing a different sort of sentence: in four days, she was due to get married—a change of status she no longer desired. So instead of having a difficult conversation, she simply disappeared from her home in Georgia. Resurfacing the following week after a nationwide manhunt had begun, she falsely claimed to have been kidnapped. The ensuing "runaway bride" media drama lasted for months.

You might imagine that there would be easier ways of dealing with problems, even serious ones. Facing criminal charges is highly stressful, but pretending to be in a coma? Claiming to be kidnapped before your wedding, instead of admitting to cold feet?

As wild as these stories are, though, perhaps they're merely extreme examples of what we might call "logically illogical" human behavior. They are responses to the kinds of cognitive distortions that we all experience.

We'll go out of our way—sometimes way out of our way—to avoid facing difficult situations. In addition to the able-bodied man pretending to be in a coma and the runaway bride, numerous people have even faked their own death to avoid a confrontation.

Just think about how hard it would be to create a convincing story of your own death. Doing so requires staged accidents, forged death certificates, and sometimes even a fake funeral service. Still, somehow, the people who do it are persuaded that going down such a convoluted path is preferable to facing the truth.

I'll Get Back to You . . . Never

As with most other subjects in this book, my interest in avoidance is not strictly academic. While I haven't faked my own death yet (I'm saving that one), I'm sorry to say that I'm all too familiar with avoidant behavior.

I began to notice this pattern early in my entrepreneurial career, when I hated talking on the phone with strangers. *Hate* is a
strong word, but it fits. For a while, I managed a service selling
gift cards. Other businesses would buy them as giveaways for
their customers.

I operated this business almost entirely online. That's not so
strange these days, but more than twenty years ago, it was still
somewhat unusual. Many times, potential customers would
send an online inquiry asking for a phone call. I always
steered them to email. Sometimes the diversion
worked, but not everyone was comfortable making a
purchase without a "real" conversation.

One time, a buyer was ready to place a large
order but wanted to talk for a few minutes
first. The money would have meant a lot to
me, but I couldn't bring myself to make the
call. I remember sitting in front of my computer with the phone in my hand, stalling for fifteen
minutes or more before giving up. I never responded to his last
message and lost the sale.*

I thought of this experience years later when a close colleague
vanished from my life without a trace. I'd known this person for
years and considered them a friend, but one day they just disappeared. To be clear, they didn't disappear from the rest of the
world, just from my world. It was obvious that I'd done something to hurt them, but I never found out what it was. What started
with slight avoidance turned into a full-blown disappearing act.

---

* I later learned that "phone anxiety" is a thing. Some people can develop a
condition known as telephobia. For others (like me), talking on the phone is
more of an aversion, where we'd generally prefer any other means of contact.

It made me sad, but I remembered my own habit of avoiding hard conversations and tried to keep this colleague's avoidance in perspective. In a way, it wasn't so strange: for many people, ghosting is now a common way of ending relationships.

Why and How We Avoid

Why do we avoid? Because it feels good, even if it doesn't help. Avoidance is rooted in our evolutionary mechanisms. *There's a threat—we should get out of the way!* Deferring something indefinitely is often the wrong choice, but it provides relief in the moment.

Avoidance is a common response to stress. We can avoid even when it makes no sense to do so and even when the pain of avoidance is greater than the pain of engagement. Avoidance tools like scrolling on your phone are easy to access and constantly available. Not only is scrolling always an option, it's endless. You can look at your phone for "just a few minutes" before bed, and half an hour easily passes.

It's not the phone's fault, though. Some form of avoidance is always available to us, even without a personal entertainment device at hand. In fact, most activities you participate in can become strategies of avoidance.

This includes things that are good for you in some circumstances but less so in others. Exercise, mindfulness, sex, walks in the woods—all such activities are sometimes helpful, and sometimes not.

You can avoid at work, at home, at school—pretty much anywhere. You can avoid in any relationship. Similarly, the consequences of avoidance can follow you everywhere. Avoidance can sabotage your job, your friendships, and your mental health.

Staying Busy Is Another Way of Avoiding

If you're not guilty of ghosting your longtime friends or failing to make simple phone calls, there's at least one more avoidance strategy that you might relate to. It's called *staying busy*.

Staying busy is one of the best ways to put off something else that you should be doing. If you're too busy to think, you're less anxious! You're on a mission—or at least you have something to do. True, it might not be the right thing, the best thing, or even a good thing, but it's something.

Have you ever noticed how some people are uncomfortable with silence? They automatically fill up any space with conversation. They experience social anxiety with long pauses, especially in closed spaces like cars or elevators.

With time anxiety, staying busy is the equivalent behavior of filling up space with conversation. You simply *have* to have something to do. So that's what happens: you go out and find it, because there are always plenty of options. This new task then takes up your time, conveniently allowing you to keep deferring whatever urgent or important tasks you should probably be doing.

The Cost of Avoidance

Like time blindness, chronic avoidance comes with a high psychological cost. Whatever short-term relief you feel comes with something to "pay back" later, because avoidant situations tend to recur.

Avoidance consumes a great deal of energy—mentally, emotionally, and physically. You might not be actively thinking about what you're avoiding, but it's usually lurking around in the back of your mind. (And by thinking you're not thinking about it, you're thinking about it. Whoa.)

Avoidance prevents you from being present, from appreciating whatever is happening right now. Similarly, chronic avoidance robs you of your ability to think clearly about the future. Dealing with the problem gets more and more difficult, or at least your perception of the problem does.

So what can be done? Start with this: *if you want to feel better, face more and avoid less.*

Face More, Avoid Less

It might sound like an easy enough task: just stop resisting. Accept the pain of facing a difficult task without dragging it out into suffering. In reality, though, it's not so simple. When it comes to putting things off, pretending they don't exist, or just ignoring reality, we'll give it all we've got.

Searching online one day, I came upon a phrase that suggested a clue to how we might stop resisting: *face everything, avoid nothing.* Could this be an anecdote of sorts?

I like that phrase—face everything, avoid nothing—but personally I find the idea of never avoiding anything to be intimidating. Instead, I try to practice a more achievable model: *face more, avoid less.*

Simply put, I'm not going to have a perfect record. But I know that when I choose to do something that's bothering me instead of continuing to put it off, I'll usually feel better—both in the moment and as an investment in my future self.

If you can't jump straight in to a big thing you're avoiding, start with something smaller. (The activity at the end of the chapter will give you a framework for this.) Some examples are:

- If you struggle with social anxiety or if it's just hard for you to talk to people, set a goal of speaking to one new person a day. Here's a trick: ask a stranger for the time, or for simple directions to somewhere nearby—even if you know the answer. These easy interactions will build up your confidence.
- Afraid of driving? Sit in the driver's seat of a parked car without going anywhere. Learn to feel comfortable with the environment and the controls.
- If you're a black-and-white thinker, try to develop flexible thinking where you adapt to new information and consider different perspectives. When you see only two choices (A or B), actively look for a third option. Even if it's not a great option, it helps you break the habit of binary thinking.
- Need to ask your boss for a recommendation because you're leaving to work another job? This might feel scary, so start the day off by asking a friend for a book or movie recommendation. Asking for other things can get you in the habit of asking before you raise the more important question.

The British man who spent two years pretending to be in a coma to avoid going to court may hold the world record for avoidance—but some of the rest of us are pretty good at it, too. We avoid because we don't see an alternative, and we like the immediate (temporary) relief it provides.

But deliberately avoiding something you really need to do has a cost. It will drain your energy even when you think you aren't thinking about it.

Real, lasting relief lies on the other side of avoidance. Identify things you're putting off indefinitely, push through or take them off your list entirely, and feel better.

PRACTICE

Write a To-Dread List

MAKE A TO-DO LIST CONSISTING OF EVERYTHING
YOU'RE PUTTING OFF.

What do you do when you're avoiding several things at once?
Simple: you make a to-dread list.

This list is exactly as it sounds. It's like a to-do list, but it contains everything you probably should do but really don't want to. That overdue email reply, that loving-but-corrective feedback you need to give to a co-worker, dealing with a bill you've been avoiding—all of those things are typical items on a to-dread list.

Of course, your list is your own. So take some time and write down whatever you can think of. Maybe you normally group items by categories like "phone calls" or "errands" or something else. Well, guess what the items on your to-dread list have in common? You don't want to do them! They deserve their own list.

Once you have the list, devote a chunk of time (perhaps half an hour, maybe longer depending on the tasks) to actively tackle only those items on the list and nothing else. You might need to schedule this into your calendar to make sure you prioritize it.

I know, it will be painful. But just remember: it's going to feel so good to get those difficult things done. Putting them off is psychologically expensive, so stop pushing them forward day after day on your to-do list. *Make a to-dread list; spend half an hour on it and feel better.*

13

Move On Quickly

AVOID "FRICTION LOOPS" AND MOVE
THROUGH THE DAY WITH EASE.

When it comes to responding to emails or other messages, I tend to be either very fast or very slow. Sometimes, people are impressed when I get back to them quickly. But I know the truth: if it doesn't happen quickly, it might not happen at all.

   This pattern is not just about responding to messages, which

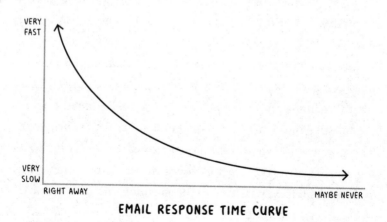

EMAIL RESPONSE TIME CURVE

typically requires some type of decision or acknowledgment. I can point to a similar pattern of getting stuck in making decisions of all kinds, even very small ones.

→ **WHAT SHOULD I EAT FOR LUNCH TODAY?**

Hmmm. I have a few go-to restaurants, but maybe I should try a new place? Or maybe I just need to eat a small snack and plan for an early dinner? So many options . . .

→ **I'D LIKE TO RELAX BY WATCHING A NEW SHOW. WHAT SHOULD I CHOOSE?**

When I open Netflix, I can spend an hour scrolling through options, reading reviews, and watching trailers. By the time I finally decide, I'm too tired to watch anything.

→ **SHOULD I PLAN TO DO SOMETHING WITH FRIENDS NEXT WEEK?**

I'd really like to see my friends, but it's hard to schedule in advance since I have no idea what the day will be like when it comes around. It's probably better to say no, just so I don't find myself feeling bad about going to something I don't want to.

(I have a hard time committing to specific times and dates, because I worry that I'm not using the time well or that "something else will be better" when the time comes.)

What's Going on Here? Friction Loops!

I call these unhelpful thought patterns *friction loops*. When I'm slow in making decisions or completing simple tasks, part of what happens is that a loop builds up. I neglect responding to messages, but since I've already read them, I'm thinking about them in the back of my mind even as I go on to other things. Or I've already spent time looking at travel options, but because I failed to make a decision, I go back to those tabs on my browser and start the process over. It's not just that this constant cycling is inefficient. It's also low-grade demoralizing.

Friction causes you to get stuck, going back and forth without making real progress. The more friction you encounter, the more time and energy you waste—resources that are already in high demand!

For example, imagine you receive an urgent request for information about something at work. A friction-loop thought pattern might look something like this:

9:00 a.m.: "Okay, there's that email from the VP about the project proposal. I should respond to this right away."

9:03 a.m.: "Hmm, but how should I phrase this? I don't want to sound too eager, but I also don't want to seem disinterested."

9:07 a.m.: "Maybe I should outline my thoughts first. Let me open a new document . . ."

9:12 a.m.: "Actually, I should probably check the latest project numbers before I respond. Where did I save that spreadsheet?"

9:18 a.m.: "These numbers look different from what I remember. I should double-check with Sarah from accounting."

9:22 a.m.: "I'll just send Sarah a quick message . . . Oh, look, another urgent email came in. I should take care of that first."

9:26 a.m.: "Okay, back to the VP's email. Where was I? Right, the project numbers. But wait, what if the VP is looking for more of a big-picture response rather than detailed numbers?"

9:29 a.m.: "Maybe I'm overthinking this. I should just write a quick, professional response. But what if I miss something important?"

9:32 a.m.: "You know what? I'll come back to this after my 10:00 a.m. meeting. I'll have a clearer head then."

Of course, by the time you return to the task, you'll need to start much of the process all over again. This costs time and energy and can lead to a sense of lose-lose: "The information might be helpful or outdated now, but if I don't reply at all, the VP will lose faith in me."

The friction in these situations often stems from an underlying fear or limiting belief, such as:

- **Perfectionism:** "I have to make the absolute best choice."
- **Fear of unknown variables:** "If I choose this, I might miss out on something better."

- **Imposter syndrome:** "Who am I to make this decision? What if I mess up?"
- **All-or-nothing thinking:** "If it's not a clear win, it must be the wrong choice."

Friction loops keep you second-guessing and spinning your wheels instead of taking purposeful action. You feel anxious and uncertain, convinced you need to think harder when what you really need is to decide and move on!

The constant cognitive reshuffling makes it hard to focus. It also contributes to time anxiety. *How should you spend your time? What should you do next?*

When you think about those questions as you continually defer small decisions, you go back to all the undone, unfinished things.

In another chapter, I'll argue that you can simply leave some of those unfinished things permanently undone. But as a general means of operation, I encourage you to move quickly through this world of small decisions. Make them, then move on.

"Ease Loops" Are the Opposite of Friction Loops

You might know that context-switching, sometimes called multi-tasking, is unhelpful and comes at a cost. This is true! But it's not just context-switching—it's failing to complete a task before making the switch. When you finish something (even something very small or simple), you can feel much better.

Accomplishing simple tasks repeatedly moves you away from a friction loop and toward its logical opposite: ease loops.

When you move quickly, instead of getting bogged down by more and more things you need to do, you build up a mental reservoir of "I did this" actions.

It's like playing a video game level that's been tough in the past, but when you return to it after a break you intuitively know exactly what to do. You race through the level and avoid every obstacle, collect every power-up, and knock out the end boss without breaking a sweat.

Again, this isn't always how it goes. But it's an ideal target to aim for.

Try to Touch Things Once

One of the best things you can do to move toward ease and away from friction is to *practice making quick decisions*. To do this, try to "touch" things you need to do one time only. For example:

- Working through emails or messages? Go through them one by one instead of picking and choosing or skipping around. Make it a game, with a small reward of doing something else after you've processed a certain number of them.
- What should you have for lunch? Think about it once, then make a decision. Deciding isn't something that needs to keep you busy for long. Or perhaps even better: decide on a healthy lunch option in advance, and make it your default choice. When you aren't sure what to eat, there's your answer.
- What should you buy for a friend's birthday? Do as much research as you truly need, but then just buy something instead of leaving it for later, when you'll likely go through the same process of searching and brainstorming.

(Note: It won't always be possible to apply the "touch things once" rule. Just work on making it more of a habit and following it whenever you can.)

What About Slow Culture?

In response to productivity culture, some people point to minimalism or "slow culture," which has a lot of different interpretations. In this case, however, slow is the problem, not the solution.

Being slow is ideal for savoring a meal with friends. Deciding on your daily lunch or your regular grocery shopping list, however, should be quick and easy.

It can be hard to see the difference between these two perspectives at first, but the more you practice quick decisions, the easier they become. You conserve energy and gain capacity you can use for far more important things.

Recover from Feeling Stuck

As noted, touching things once is not a one-and-done habit (even though you're trying to only touch things once!). Most likely, you'll experience a pattern of ebb and flow with friction and ease. One thing that helps when you get stuck: *focus on the next right step.*

Friction comes from trying to map the entire path. Ease is taking one step at a time. Ask yourself, "What's one small action I can take to move forward?" then do that action. Doing so puts you back on an ease track.

It can also help to streamline recurring decisions, thus getting rid of the need to make them over and over. This is why some people prepare their meals for the week in advance, or preselect outfits, or otherwise "batch" tasks so they're out of the way for several days or weeks at a time. (The fewer variables involved, the less friction you'll encounter.)

Friction loops grind us down, while ease loops give us a boost. We want to move toward ease and away from friction.

PRACTICE

The Confirm Button Never Disappoints

THINKING OF BOOKING A FLIGHT, HOTEL STAY,
OR SOMETHING ELSE ONLINE? HERE'S A CRAZY IDEA:
JUST BOOK IT.

Back when I traveled all the time, I also spent several hours each week making travel plans. I would constantly go back and forth over the various options, sometimes becoming plagued by indecision. The FOMO was real.

My friend Stephanie also traveled a lot—and while we were both pretty experienced, she was better at booking for one key reason: *she'd learned to be decisive*. I asked her how to explain her process, which mostly came down to "stop overthinking so much."

Here's how she put it:

> I waste a lot of time on minor decisions because I want the best thing. But the truth is that there isn't always a best thing—or perhaps there are several best things. At the end of the day it probably doesn't matter which hotel I stay at or how I arrive from the airport.
>
> When you make a decision, you can move on with the rest of the planning. But until you make the decision, you can't move on.

I've thought about Stephanie's model—she also calls it "just book the fucking ticket"—many times since then, usually when

I feel myself wasting time refreshing itinerary options and opening new browser tabs to check on yet another idea.

You know how when you're buying something online, there's that final confirmation button after making an initial selection? It feels really good to stop hesitating and click that button. The confirm button never disappoints.

14

Not Finishing Things Is
One of the Great Joys of Life

TO SAVE TIME AND FEEL GREATLY RELIEVED,
STOP TRYING TO FINISH EVERYTHING.

Another false belief you may have assimilated at some point without much thought is that everything you start needs to be finished.

In fact, many things can be abandoned! And you'll be much better off if you practice the habit of "un-finishing."

For example, I know people who commit to finish every book they start to read, no matter what they think of it. To each their own—but personally I think this is a mistake. There are many, many great books in the world. Far more, in fact, than you could ever read, even if you narrow the list down to your absolute favorites.

Why then would you force yourself to keep slogging along with one that isn't working for you? Much better to stop and move on to another that you might enjoy much more.

The same logic applies to all forms of media and entertainment: TV, movies, games, and so on. There's a lot of good stuff out there—don't give too much time to anything that doesn't feel worth it anymore, even if you've already started it.

Not Finishing Doesn't Mean You Hated It

Un-finishing doesn't only apply when you dislike something. Maybe you learned all you needed from that book in the first few chapters. Maybe that TV series was great for the first season, but it really didn't need to go on forever. You enjoyed it until you stopped enjoying it, and that is the time for you to *stop watching it*. Instead of binge-watching, appreciate the memory of what it was for a while.

By adopting this practice, you'll experience two amazing benefits. First, you'll save an incredible amount of time. Even if you're a fast reader, it will take you an average of four hours to read a three-hundred-page book. Stop fifty pages in if it's not working for you, and you get back three hours of your life. The fifth season of the show that started so well but then just kept humming along, rehashing the same plots with slightly different characters? Another nine hours.

.   .   .

The second amazing benefit is that walking away from things leads to feeling incredibly free. If you're used to the habit of always trying to finish what you've started, it might seem strange at first to un-finish, like you're skipping school or otherwise being naughty. You might expect to feel bad, since dropping out early isn't what you've been accustomed to.

But soon thereafter, you'll feel better—much better, in fact. You'll be proud of yourself for trusting your intuition and moving on.

This is especially true for anything that has a financial cost attached, like walking out of a movie that you're seeing in a theater. Sure, you paid for it—but that doesn't matter if you don't like it. Be bold! By leaving early, you're buying back time for yourself to spend on something else.

Cutting Things Short Also Applies to Social Situations

Adopt and adapt this principle wherever you can in life, not just to books and TV, but anywhere you can move on from something that's not enjoyable or helpful to you. Leave boring parties early. Excuse yourself from unproductive meetings. (Note to parents: of course you want to be present for your children, but do you need to attend every one of their after-school and sporting activities? For some families, this attendance becomes a very demanding part-time job.)

I understand that moving on quickly is harder in social situations, but the more you can un-finish something, the more you'll experience the two benefits (more time and more pride in your ability to value what you enjoy).

One thing that might help you move on quickly is to strategically avoid situations where it's hard to un-finish. A friend of mine went on an online dating kick a few months after a divorce.

She wasn't entirely sure what she was looking for, so she wanted to meet a lot of people to find out.

It was an interesting experiment, and she learned something early on: dinner and a movie (or sometimes just dinner!) is way too long for a first date. She started meeting her dates for an early evening walk that began with picking up a to-go coffee or tea. Going for a walk made the process feel more active, instead of just sitting across from a stranger in a restaurant, and it also came with an intuitive timetable of an hour or less.

If she—and the other person, of course—were enjoying the vibe, they could always extend the date into dinner. But if not, the date could logically conclude after the walk, my friend could say goodnight, and then she could move on with her life. She didn't feel trapped into spending more time with the person than she wanted, and she didn't feel rude in concluding their time together.

Do yourself a great favor and learn to un-finish. You'll save time and build self-confidence. You might even find that un-finishing becomes one of your favorite habits.

PRACTICE

Walk Away Now

ABANDON ACTIVITIES THAT YOU DON'T ENJOY, AND LEAVE
EARLY FROM ENGAGEMENTS THAT NO LONGER SERVE YOU.

The world is filled with beautiful experiences. Abandon things
that are no longer making you happy, and explore something
different.

Part I: Reevaluate Your Current Engagements

Consider the media you're currently consuming. What are you
reading right now? What TV shows and movies are you watching, and what games are you playing? What websites do you
browse out of habit every day?

If you love all these things, great! But if you find you're merely
doing them out of habit, or just because they seemed good a
while back, maybe something else would be better.

*Make it a habit to reassess and move on from anything that
doesn't add value to your life.*

Part II: Practice the Art of Leaving Early

Extend this un-finishing mindset to other areas of your life. If
you're at a party that isn't enjoyable, give yourself permission
to leave. At a restaurant with a menu you don't like? Find a better place. I don't mean "Eat there now and go somewhere else

next time." I mean—just get up and go! It's not worth your time to stay.

There are always other options. By moving on from activities that don't bring you happiness, you reclaim time for those that do.

Let go of the belief that you must finish everything you start. Instead, you can "buy back" the time you would've spent and put it toward something more enjoyable.

15

Knitting Is Good for You

COZY HOBBIES LIKE KNITTING, CRAFTING,
AND PLAYING BOARD GAMES CAN LOWER YOUR
ANXIETY AND INCREASE YOUR ATTENTION SPAN.

While some of my childhood was less than idyllic, I was fortunate to grow up with grandparents who cared for me. Some of my best early memories are of working with my grandma in her garden. We also spent hours playing all sorts of board and card games, sometimes with other family members, but often with just the two of us.

I couldn't help but think of her when I heard about *granny hobbies,* which are pretty much exactly what they sound like: activities like knitting, baking, and gardening that you might sometimes associate with older people. These tactile, repetitive activities can bring us into a flow state where time seems to feel more expansive—the opposite of a perceived time shortage.

I first learned of granny hobbies from a post by Anu Atluru, a doctor, artist, and inventor (!) who writes essays in her spare time. Anu notes that some people may not like the phrase granny hobby—but to her, it's meant to be charming. Besides, the whole point of prescribing "old people activities" to youth is because maybe those grandmas are on to something.

Feeling flustered? Perhaps you should try knitting—or at least some sort of tactile, analog craft that can be easily started and stopped whenever you need.

Hands-On, Thumbs-Down

Anu describes most granny hobbies as being "hands-on, thumbs-down," meaning that you need to use your hands, but you aren't scrolling on a device. (Granted, you probably use your thumbs for these activities as well, but the point is they are phone-free.)

Granny hobbies are also low-intensity, meaning that they're easy to pick up and put down. You get better as you practice, but you can learn the basics of most of them pretty quickly. The skills you acquire through one craft tend to be somewhat transferable to others, allowing you to more easily try out new things.

Finally, these cozy hobbies also have relatively low stakes. If you're learning to bake and you burn a cake in the oven, oh well. You haven't deleted a database or cc'd the entire company on the wrong email. You can simply try again, either the same day or whenever you feel like coming back to it later.

Granny Hobbies Aren't Just Fun, They're Also Good for You

A story in *The New York Times* referred to two recent studies that found hobbies such as knitting, gardening, and coloring were associated with cognitive improvements related to both memory and attention—and a reduction in symptoms of anxiety and depression. It's hard to beat that!

Granny hobbies also offer a small area of control and mastery. Accepting that many things are outside your control can be helpful, as we looked at a few chapters ago. But it's also nice to be able to have something you have complete control over and that you get better at over time. Most granny hobbies fit this description perfectly.

. . .

Thinking about granny hobbies reminded me of people I know who are into home remodeling, serious woodworking, or otherwise building things in their spare time. These days, many of us spend much of our time at a desk in front of a screen. If you don't work in a trade, it might be fulfilling to explore one of these tactile hobbies.

I also heard a reverse version of this practice from a guy in Canada who works as a carpenter but started a side project involving computer work. Before he switched to carpentry, he was a graphic designer and found that he missed that type of work.

Both of these approaches point to a general guideline: it might be good to do something substantially different for your extra-hours projects (or just your hobbies) than you do for your day job.

Social or Solitary

Another fun thing about most granny hobbies is that you can do them on your own *or* with others. There are benefits both ways. If you're seeking companionship—perhaps with like-minded people who are also interested in putting down their phones for a while—look for a group organized around one of the crafts.

"Game nights" that feature board, card, or tabletop games take place in most cities every week. Often, retail stores will host groups for different activities: a puzzle store for puzzle night, a yarn shop for knitting club, and so on.

If you're looking for one, search online for "game night" or "puzzle night" in your area. You might find additional options by looking on Meetup.com or Reddit.

Afraid to go on your own? Send a message to the organizer ahead of time, and they'll help you get connected. Worried you won't be good enough? You certainly don't need to be an expert. The whole point of these groups is *community*. Book clubs aren't really about the book, and knitting groups aren't just about knitting.

And of course, you don't have to turn any of these hobbies into a social experience. If your life is already full of enough social interactions, you may prefer to pursue your crafts in peace and quiet. Not only are granny hobbies low-intensity, they're also low-commitment. You can return to them whenever you need a break from the rest of life's busyness.

Try Out a Granny Hobby

Getting started is a simple process. First, select a granny hobby of your choice! Among others, the list of possibilities could include:

quilting, birdwatching, puzzling, candle making, flower art, genealogy, cooking, calligraphy, knitting or crocheting, photography, woodworking, pottery or ceramics, drawing, gardening, board or card games, mahjong, scrapbooking, sewing, reading, journaling, collecting, baking, needlepoint, crafting, and painting

Remember, the key features of these hobbies are *hands-on, thumbs-down* (no scrolling on devices), and *low-intensity*, meaning that the stakes are low and you can work on them or set them aside for long periods of time.

Next, make a plan to get started. Every granny hobby has a large ecosystem of teachers and practitioners. YouTube is full of detailed, free videos you can watch to learn. Most instruction is aimed at beginners, so you'll be right at home. You can also visit a local craft shop, which, in addition to hosting events, will be happy to help you build a starter pack of items you need.

This is a bigger lift, but you might also want to consider a whole year's worth of cozy hobbies, with a new form or format every month:

January: Pottery

February: Candle making

March: Crochet

And so on.

What's so special about tactile, nondigital acts? There's something about the repetitive, low-key action that just feels good. When you fall in with the right granny hobby, time tends to pass differently. It's a hyperfocus of its own, but perhaps a bit softer than the hyperfocus we feel during an intense work rush.

You might be familiar with fidget spinners, or just fidgets in general. These are typically small, handheld objects that you can manipulate with your fingers, often repetitively. The visual and tactile feedback they provide can be soothing or satisfying.

Well, guess what? Many granny hobbies also feature the ultimate fidgets! Some of them, like knitting and needlepoint, are also highly portable. Not only can you easily start, pause, and resume them, you can also do them wherever you are.

From reduced anxiety to increased cognitive attention, there's a lot to like about these activities. In a world of constant pressure and time scarcity, maybe a granny hobby is what we all need.

PRACTICE

Pack Portable Items for a Tactile Break

WHETHER YOU GO ALL IN ON A GRANNY HOBBY OR NOT, CONSIDER A PORTABLE ACTIVITY YOU CAN TAKE WITH YOU FOR DOWNTIME OUTSIDE YOUR HOME.

Give your eyes and mind a rest from screens by always having a hands-on activity with you. It could be:

- A small knitting kit
- A Sudoku or other puzzle book
- A fidget of some kind
- A journal of some kind
- Something else!

Whatever you choose, store it in a convenient place (like by the door, for example, or with your keys or handbag) so that you'll remember to take it with you when you go.

Then, instead of automatically scrolling on your phone the next time you have a short break, try replacing some of that time with your new hands-on activity.

GREEN

YELLOW

RED

16

The Traffic Light Model of Focus and Fatigue

WHY YOU SOMETIMES HAVE THE WORK ENERGY
OF A BORDER COLLIE, AND OTHER TIMES
YOU FEEL LIKE A SLOTH.

I was really excited to work on this thing last week, but today I have zero motivation for it.

. . .

I'm able to focus for hours at a time while playing a game or watching movies, but I'm unable to apply this power to work I need to finish.

. . .

Some days, I can get so much done. Other days, I struggle to do very basic things.

Do scenarios like the ones above feel familiar to you? It's frustrating to struggle with varying levels of energy and motivation—and it's a problem that most productivity methods won't help you with.

I'd like to introduce you to the hyperfocus-burnout cycle. You may have been operating by it for years without knowing what it is. As with time blindness, this cycle is especially applicable for those with ADHD—but it's also relevant for anyone else who wonders why they're sometimes very motivated to work on something and other times find it extremely difficult to make even basic progress.

As you might guess from the name, the hyperfocus-burnout cycle consists of two elements, *hyperfocus* and *burnout*.

HYPERFOCUS: Deep, prolonged attention on a task, which sometimes leads to you losing track of time

BURNOUT: A state of exhaustion from chronic stress, which reduces your motivation and productivity

The hyperfocus-burnout cycle is often described negatively, as something to be avoided. One definition I found said this:

The hyperfocus-burnout cycle **is a productivity trap** where intense, uninterrupted work sessions can lead to remarkable short-term achievements but ultimately result in physical and mental exhaustion. To avoid this, always step away from work sessions before they become too intense.

But here is a great example of how what might be true for some people isn't true for others. It's quite normal for many of us to draw on hyperfocus to work effectively. Those "remarkable achievements," even if short-term, are worth celebrating. Besides, hyperfocus times can also be fun! If you get excited about something and want to go all in on it for a while, why wouldn't you?

A better way is simply to understand the cycle and *learn to replace burnout with rest*. The mistake is to assume you can constantly hyperfocus. That's not possible—so instead, you need to allow for periods of rest in between periods of intense hyperfocus. To learn how to do that, consider the model of a traffic light's colors.

The Traffic Light Strategy

When you draw on your hyperfocus powers—with the awareness that using them will also tire you out sooner or later—picture a traffic light system. You've got three "zones" to operate in.

Green: You're in a state of flow or hyperfocus, working efficiently and effectively. You're energized, engaged, and productive, similar to a green light indicating it's safe to go.

When you're in this zone—live it up! Just be mindful of distractions, because you can easily end up hyperfocusing on something less helpful or useful.

Yellow: You're approaching a danger zone. While you're able to complete some tasks, you might be neglecting signs of fatigue or overwork. The yellow zone is a warning to slow down, take breaks, and reassess your workload to prevent slipping into the red zone. Easy does it.

Red: You've hit your limit. Productivity declines as exhaustion, both physical and mental, takes over. Like a red traffic light, this zone indicates a stop: you need to rest, recover, and reevaluate before returning to the green zone. Trying to work intensely during red-zone times is counterproductive.

You can experience these changing zones in a short time period, like a single hour of focused work, but it might be more helpful to think about entire days of green, yellow, or red. Some days feel different than others, right? You have strong days, average days, and days where getting even simple things done is difficult.

If you think about traffic lights in your life, some obvious lessons might emerge. Here's an important one: evaluate yourself on a longer time horizon.

Evaluate Yourself on a Longer Time Horizon

Any particular day might go off course. Traffic turns into a mess, an urgent situation comes up, or you're forced to redirect the attention you so eagerly planned to devote to your favorite project. Because not everything is within our control, we can't guarantee that any given day will be full of green-light energy.

Hey, it happens!

It might not even be outside circumstances that derail you. Your energy level is determined by biological factors including hormones, nutrition, and age. For all these reasons and more, judging yourself on a day-to-day basis is unhelpful.

Therefore, stop judging yourself by your days—take the view of a longer time horizon. Enlarge the sample size of available data. Consider weekly, monthly, or even longer evaluations of your work and life. Here's a principle we'll come to later: *you overestimate what you can do in a day, but you underestimate what you can do over longer periods of time.*

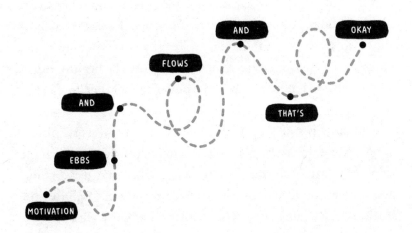

This principle also suggests some advice for parents who feel guilty about not raising their kids as perfectly as they might have imagined. Maybe you let your kid eat three candy bars today, or an important work meeting led you to miss an after-school activity. But are you more or less doing your best to raise them well? Okay, then. These experiences will even out over time.

In addition, looking at longer cycles of time is helpful for something else. As an ADHD coach explained to me, one of her big goals is to help people allow themselves to rest on those red or yellow days. They feel like they "can't" or "shouldn't" rest—but if they zoom out and see how productive they are on the green days, they're more likely to give themselves permission.

Rest Will Come Whether You Want It Or Not

Rest periods away from hyperfocus mode are not optional. Your body needs rest, so it will take it one way or another—but rest is also a lot like sleep itself. You have to sleep, like it or not, but there are ways to *sleep better*.

You could drag yourself kicking and screaming to bed every night, scrolling on your phone until you fall asleep watching short videos, or you can develop a healthy sleep ritual that prepares your body for sleep.[*] When you choose the healthy ritual, you usually feel more rested in the morning and therefore better prepared for your day.

The same is true with taking rest periods from work. You're simply not going to be able to work in hyperfocus mode all the time (so, start by acknowledging this). When you feel anxious about time, you tend to restrict yourself from rest. Cognitive distortions that challenge your ability to rest might include:

"I have to get up an hour earlier tomorrow, because there's so much that isn't done."

"If I just drink more caffeine, I can power through."

"I need to work smarter AND harder!"

This kind of tough love self-talk is usually unhelpful, at least

---

[*] My ritual changes from time to time, but it typically consists of: limiting food, TV, and gaming after 8:00 p.m. and then drinking a magnesium beverage while reading for an hour before bed.

as anything other than a rare exception. Your body needs rest, just like it needs oxygen and water.

One way or another, rest will come to you. It's better to welcome and plan for it than to end up in a state of exhaustion.

What to Do on Yellow Days

Okay, so you might understand what to do in a green-light or red-light situation. Green means go! Red means stop. But what about yellow?

This middle ground can be confusing, not just in terms of your ability to do cognitively intense work. It turns out that yellow traffic lights—as in, the ones on the streets—are tricky, too.

As part of renewing my driver's license, I recently learned that yellow-light laws can vary by state and region. Some states are "permissive yellow," which means that drivers approaching a yellow light can safely proceed through it, as long as they clear the intersection before it turns red. Others are "restrictive yellow," which means the opposite—drivers are required to stop on yellow unless it's unsafe to do so. Meanwhile, many other states simply don't specify their yellow-light laws. Be careful on your next cross-country road trip!

Getting back to hyperfocus and burnout: here's what to do on your yellow-light days.

1. Lower the goal of output.

If you can't take it easy on a yellow day, at least take it *easier*. Whatever your work quota is, try to dial it down. If you can normally do five big tasks on a green-light day, for example, plan to do only two on a yellow-light day.

(Recall the exercise "What does done look like?" from Chapter 8, where you decide for yourself what the end point of any task will be.)

2. Do something different.

Work on something else! You might be able to get a full green-light day's worth of cognitive effort on a yellow-light day if you work on something different than what you've been doing. Yellow-light days can be great for side hustles or other unrelated projects. You don't have to take it easy the whole day (and, of course, you might not able to)—just be careful, because you're still not operating at peak capacity. Yellow does not mean "mostly green."

3. Push through (but be prepared to pay the cost).

Sometimes, depending on the circumstances of your work and nonwork life, you just have to go for it. It happens! Just don't expect to do this often or without consequences.

For many years I hosted a weeklong annual event for more than a thousand people. My small team and I were extremely busy that week.

There was no other way around it. Each one of us had a lot of responsibility for the event, and we really wanted to make people happy for the week they were in town.

But at the end of the weekend, we crashed hard. It took a few days for everyone to recover, and we learned to avoid scheduling anything important or pressing during those days. Fortunately, we then had several months to do other things before beginning a new planning cycle for the next year's event.

For those times where you must push through, be as gentle on yourself as possible once you reach the other side.

• • •

Hyperfocus can be fun, so don't be afraid to lean into it. At the same time, hyperfocus creates a biological need for rest and recovery, so be sure to plan for it.

Understanding the hyperfocus-burnout cycle leads to a strategy you can use to work more effectively and feel less anxious about the times when you're being "less productive."

Finally, stop evaluating yourself based on a single day. Some days will end up falling apart, despite your best efforts. Consider all you do over the course of a longer time cycle, however, and see if you don't feel differently about yourself.[*]

Used sparingly, hyperfocus can be a powerful tool. Just don't expect to work in hyperfocus mode all the time, because it will lead to burnout and more time anxiety.

---

[*] Thanks to Nicole Bulsara for sharing the traffic light analogy with me.

PRACTICE

"What Matters to Me Right Now?"

STOP AND ASK YOURSELF WHAT'S IMPORTANT IN THIS MOMENT.

Just like paying active attention, simply taking inventory of what's truly important can work wonders. It can serve as a jump start for changing up your work (i.e., trying to reprioritize or switching gears to do something different), or it can merely be an observation point you take note of. Here's how you do it.

In the midst of a busy day, or when you're feeling overwhelmed with a bunch of things being thrown at you all at once, simply pause for a moment.

Take a few deep breaths.

Then, ask yourself: *What matters to me right now?*

Your answer should be fairly intuitive (you'll know it when you think about it), but allow thirty seconds to pass as you fully reflect on the question.

Whatever your answer is, it may cause you to rethink your to-do list. It may lead you to go off autopilot and into a deeper mode of focused work. It may lead you to step away from work altogether for a few minutes or hours. Or, of course, it may not do any of those things. After reflecting on the question, if your answer is "Exactly what I'm doing right now," that's great. Keep doing that.

17

A Light Schedule Is Sometimes Harder than a Full One

WHY WE SOMETIMES FEEL MORE OVERWHELMED
WHEN WE'RE LESS BUSY.

Tania, a professional voice actor from Los Angeles, told me she was having trouble understanding where her time goes.

"Did you always feel this way," I asked her, "or has it been more pronounced since the pandemic?"

"Kind of always," she said. "Maybe more since the pandemic, but here's the weird thing. I used to have to pack everything in to a busy schedule. Now I have a lot of time, and I'm more stressed out."

It's another strange pattern in our relationship with time that doesn't make sense at first. If you have more free time, shouldn't you be more relaxed? Yet sometimes your emotions work the other way: *having a light schedule can feel more stressful than a full one.*

I've noticed this correlation especially with people who are newly self-employed. Sometimes their side business is going so well that they take the leap and quit their day job to work fully on their own. They imagine that they'll have "so much more time" once they no longer have to answer to someone else.

But as you've probably guessed, the opposite occurs. Instead of growing their business with all the extra hours in their schedule, they can end up stalling. The first few days feel great, or maybe even the first couple of weeks, but after a while the great freedom of owning so much time turns into an unexpected burden.

Don't get me wrong: having more free time is better than having less. If your schedule is so jam-packed that you don't have time to breathe, you end up running on fumes. But just because this alternative is preferable doesn't mean it's without issues.

For many of us, it's the biggest problem of our lives: out of countless options, how do we best use the time we have?

You Have a Natural Limit on Daily Productive Hours

In the book *Daily Rituals*, Mason Currey documented the life and work patterns of famous people, including Mozart, Beethoven, Tolstoy, and many others. One of the biggest takeaways from Currey's research was that *most people are able to do no more than three to four hours of focused work per day.* Even prolific writers and artists (Charles Dickens, Maya Angelou, Pablo Picasso, and others) were rarely able to work through the whole day. Their specific routines varied, but a common pattern among them was a few hours of concentrated work in the morning, followed by pretty much anything other than focused work.

Dickens took long walks through the city, an act that improved his powers of observation and was integral to his creativity. Beethoven worked much the same way, rising at 6:00 a.m. and counting out exactly sixty beans for his morning coffee—perhaps a sign of great attention to detail. After a work session in a spartan office (no distractions!), he took off for lunch and an extended walk in the Viennese woods. Though he returned to work for editing after the break, he viewed the long interruption as essential to his process.

• • •

To go back to the example of newly self-employed people, one of the mistakes they make is to imagine that they can seriously ramp up their productive time. It makes sense, in a way: they figure that they've been "cramming" their side hustle or after-hours business into a concentrated period of time. Now, with more time available, they're going to crush it!

The problem is that they've likely been doing this concentrated work in a highly effective way that can't magically be multiplied to fill many additional hours throughout the day.

So if they go from working on their project from one hour a day to eight hours a day, it's almost certain that they won't be eight times more effective. Perhaps they can double their output, which should be seen as a huge win. But they shouldn't usually try to do what they were doing before, only maximized for a much longer period of time.

Of course, you may be thinking, "But I have a job that requires my availability for more than three to four hours a day."

Yes! But the limitation is on focused work that requires a high level of cognitive attention—that's what is generally unable to sustain itself throughout the day.

The ability to concentrate comes with a built-in limitation. You can still do things throughout a full work day, but if you want to be effective, you need to intersperse those concentrated tasks with different things.

Learn to Manage Yourself, Not Time

Once you understand the natural limit of daily productive hours, it probably makes more sense why having more free time can feel more stressful or overwhelming than a compressed schedule.

The wrong thing to do in response to this realization is to start padding out your schedule, just because doing so is a familiar, comfortable pattern. Much better to learn to manage yourself within this constraint—and then use the rest of the time for other things!

There are a few options for how you can do this:

- **"Work the way you used to" but in the new schedule.**
  Don't think of a day in eight-hour chunks. Imagine
  that you have a much more limited time to complete
  your most important tasks. Ideally, try to tackle these
  tasks first thing in the morning, or at least as soon as
  you can after starting a work period.
- **Alternatively, introduce new routines.** You don't have
  to work the same hours you did before—so what would
  be most productive for you? When free time is abundant,
  design a schedule around your ideal working hours.
- **Use "power hours" wisely.** Even though a majority of

people are most productive in the morning, this isn't universally true. And of course, you may have schedule restraints that are outside your control. The goal is: wherever possible, protect your power hours and use them for tasks that require the most brain power.

- **Treat healthy habits with the same level of commitment that you have for your work.** Whether you've just quit your day job or otherwise have a much lighter schedule than you used to, this is a big change. Try to maintain other healthy habits while you adjust. Don't neglect simple things like staying hydrated, moving around a lot, and eating meals.

A light schedule can be more psychologically challenging than a full one—but it doesn't have to be. Don't be afraid to put some parameters around your schedule that serve your needs. In fact, you might want to try deliberately creating built-in constraints. Consider this question:

If you <u>had</u> to radically reduce your time spent on something, how would you handle it?

I started thinking about this question when I had a bad case of the flu that lasted more than a week. I spent a good portion of each day sleeping—and probably a fair amount of each day complaining about being sick.

Of course, I still had to work some of the time. My energy level was constantly low, but every so often I'd muster enough strength to plow through a few tasks or half-heartedly reply to messages before crashing on the couch for another long nap.

No need to get sick to triage your work so severely, of course.

You can just decide that you only have a certain amount of time to work on something—and then decide how to best use the limited time. When you have clear constraints, you tend to eliminate a lot of superfluous activities.

You can also consider this thought exercise with nonwork activities or with any other amount of time. What if you had to fit in a workout in less than fifteen minutes? What if you had to plan a big trip, and instead of researching options for weeks, you gave yourself a two-day deadline to have everything booked?

You get the idea: limitations and constraints can be helpful. If your day isn't naturally designed around a set schedule, create the order you need to thrive.

The amount of time available to us is not the only factor that makes us feel busy or overwhelmed. Sometimes, a light schedule feels more constrictive than a full one.

PRACTICE

Review How You Spend Unscheduled Time

ANALYZE YOUR FREE TIME TO BECOME MORE
INTENTIONAL ABOUT HOW YOU SPEND IT,
WITHOUT OBSESSING OVER EVERY MINUTE.

"The time you enjoy wasting is not wasted time" is another old saying. That logic seems fair, but what about all the time where you have no idea where it went?

When I talk with people about time anxiety, they often seem puzzled about this missing time. "I know I lose a lot of minutes throughout the day, but I don't know where they go," is a common statement. One solution to this problem is to use a simple tracking system to uncover the answers. If you've never tried this before, it can be insightful.

With or without a system, however, you can likely find some activities to trim from your life that will free up time. After practicing "time decluttering" and pruning your calendar of scheduled events (see the activity in Chapter 1, page 5), you may want to look at how you spend unscheduled time.

Unscheduled time refers to those pockets of your day that aren't explicitly allocated to specific tasks or appointments. This could include time spent scrolling through social media, waiting for something to start, or simply zoning out. It's the time that often slips by without us realizing it.

To review this time, try keeping a log for a few days. Jot down how you spend your unstructured time, even if it's just for ten-minute intervals. Be honest with yourself—the goal isn't to judge but to understand.

You might notice patterns—like reaching for your phone whenever you have a spare moment or spending a lot of time on activities that don't align with your priorities.

Some people find they're engaging in "time confetti"—scattering their attention across many small, often unproductive activities. Others might realize they're spending significant time on one particular activity they hadn't consciously chosen to prioritize.

Important: The goal of this exercise isn't to micromanage every minute of your day or to eliminate all leisure time. It's simply to show that you might have more free time than you think.

Just as it's not a single donut that contributes to obesity, one unplanned minute doesn't contribute to time loss. When reviewing your unscheduled time, you want to focus on large blocks of time that don't contribute positively to your life. Don't worry about optimizing every ten minutes; that will just make you more anxious.

To do more of what matters, something else has to go—not for the sake of doing less, but because time is limited and you want to spend as much of it as possible doing something you find meaningful.

A Short Summary of Part 2

Time itself doesn't change, but our perception of time does. At different ages, you experience the same amount of time in different ways.

Avoiding hard things can feel good temporarily, but avoidance comes with a lingering psychological cost. Make a to-dread list of the things you're avoiding, and set aside thirty minutes to do only those things. Be prepared to feel much better (and for much longer) afterward.

Learning to move quickly through the world—or at least through tasks of lesser consequence—can help you free up time and space for more important things.

Classic hobbies like knitting (and many others) that are tactile and low-stakes can feel surprisingly freeing. They can give you a sense of control and mastery, and can be done socially or on your own.

Periods of intense work (sometimes called *hyperfocus*) can be very helpful! We just need to remember that it's not possible to work at the same pace all the time. Balance periods of hyperfocus with deliberate periods of rest.

Most of us have a natural cap of three to four hours of focused work per day. Learn to work with this limitation instead of fighting it.

INTERLUDE

On the Lack of Success in Duplicating the Productivity Patterns of Famous World Leaders

You say you are writing a book about time anxiety. But what will it include? What advice will you offer? You worry that despite your intimate relationship with this topic, you have nothing to say. *Life is hard and then it ends.* This is true! But is this logic helpful?

Elena writes you from Paris. She is a documentary filmmaker who has won many awards. She speaks around the world at conferences and companies. She posts regularly on social media. She also has a two-year-old, who is learning to speak three languages at once. Elena wants to know if you're doing any more time-anxiety courses? She'd like to join—but what, you wonder, could you teach her.

This is what it has come to: a reckoning of sorts. People always thought you were "so productive," but you know many people who are much *more* productive. You are impressed with them and also a little mad about their productivity. You think about them when you're supposed to be working on something but end up doing anything other than what you should be working on. Instead of time anxiety, you should write the book on status envy. Working title: *The Art of Looking to Others for Validation and Going Away Feeling Depressed.*

NARRATOR 1: Should it be *The Lost Art . . .* ?

NARRATOR 2: No. This art has never been far from view.

Perhaps there is one thing you can offer: most of the people you know who are more productive than you are also pretty stressed out. Some more than others, of course, but a general rule is that the more you learn about a famous productive person, the more you see that not everything is as it seems. Maybe something is going well in their world, but something else is falling apart. Maybe they're so high-strung that everyone in their presence walks around on pins and needles.

The less charitable thing to say would be the more you get to know them, the less impressed you are. But you know that the problem is not them! It's the pedestal they are placed upon in your mind. And to be fair, the one they try to maintain their position upon gets their own wheels spinning and causes them to wonder: *How should I spend my time? There's something I should be doing right now, but I don't know what it is.*

That's right. They have this problem, too.

For many years you produced an annual event with keynote speakers. Every year, you dealt with the same problem. You had confirmed these speakers in advance, and you had a copy of their travel plans. You were pretty sure they'd show up. But until you had them in the greenroom backstage, waiting to walk out and give their keynote, you never really knew. Though some were incredibly reliable, others were, well, more like you. Push comes to shove, they usually delivered. But you still worried! Because you had seen what the audience hadn't: sometimes these special people got as stressed out as you did.

You read an article about an American politician known for her books on "miracles" and mindfulness. It turns out she is also known by her staff as dehumanizing, abusive, and frequently enraged. The article alleges that she has thrown a phone at a staff member, criticized staff for their weight and physical appearance, and once punched a car door so hard that her hand required medical attention. In a response to these allegations, she denies some of the charges but admits others. She also says she is "not running for sainthood."

Carl Jung said that everyone has a shadow. The less your shadow is integrated within yourself—and the more you try to hide it—the darker it becomes.

The article about the politician ends with a quote from a disillusioned staffer, who offers the advice "Never meet your heroes." You think about the times you've been disappointed in someone you met. Then you think about the times it went the other way, when you were the one to disappoint someone who met their hero. The other person went away with the shock that their hero was just an ordinary person worried about all the things he hadn't done.

• • •

You did not write a book called *Atomic Habits*. You do not have *x* number of Instagram followers. Your special on Netflix will not be debuting next month, be sure to tell your friends and click the Like button.

You understand that Barack Obama was able to simplify his decision-making process by wearing the same type and color of suit each day. Yet when you try the same approach, simplifying your wardrobe and selecting the next day's outfit before going to bed, it does not yield the same effect that it does for a president. You do not wake up in the Oval Office, ready to handle the affairs of a nation. You wonder if this shopworn anecdote about Obama's suit-wearing holds up at all. Even if a president knows in advance what he's going to wear, doesn't he still face a multitude of additional, much more complex decisions? No, this life hack will not solve your decision fatigue.

Nor will the apps, the subscriptions you pay for, the email newsletters. Drugs, AI, the disturbingly accurate algorithms that bring personalized content direct to your handheld device—these things are neither the solution nor the problem. They are sometimes good, sometimes bad, and always extraneous. Peripheral. Symptomatic. An endless side note to the core question.

Question: *How will you choose to spend your time?*

Meaning: there is a running series of exclusive choices that do not allow you to have it all.

Because: time is running out, and this truth is stressful to contemplate.

Sometimes you must lose the battle to win the war, or at least lose now to fight another day. On some of these losing days you must accept that you will accomplish zero of the seventeen items on your list. You do not complete the latest social media fitness challenge. You share a post about vulnerability, but no one likes it. *The New York Times* does not ask you for comment.

The serenity prayer, offered in Alcoholics Anonymous and other addiction groups, asks for help to accept the things we cannot change, courage to change the things we can, and the wisdom to know the difference. Your mission is similar: to surrender in the war against time, to fight a few well-chosen battles along the way, and to gain the insight to know the difference.

PART 3

Owning Your Time

You have the power to align your time with your deepest values and purpose. Imagine balancing dreaming and doing, thinking in longer time periods, and calibrating the cadence of how you spend your days. This section helps you create space for pleasure, leisure, novelty, and fulfillment—the elements that make life more meaningful.

The meaning of life is that it stops.

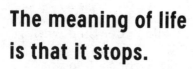

—FRANZ KAFKA

18

The Movie of Your Life

IF YOUR LIFE WAS A MOVIE AND YOU WERE THE
DIRECTOR, WHAT SCENES WOULD YOU ADD TO IT?

Imagine you're watching a feature-length movie that tells the story of your life. It's not an abridged documentary—it's a detailed view of your full life story, complete with highlights, lowlights, and everything in between.

Now imagine that you're the director of this extended production. As the person in charge, you have final say over what goes in and what stays out.

Good film editors know that every scene exists for a reason. So if you had the chance to watch the movie of your life up to this point—the one you directed—you might wonder why you chose to add certain scenes to it.

What was your character's motivation? Was there something hidden or unseen that took place in parallel to whatever was happening on-screen? What can you learn from those editing decisions?

Watching the rough cut of your movie should make you feel proud. Sure, there are probably some embarrassing moments—we all have them—but also, sometimes you really crushed it! These special memories, accomplishments, relationships, times you cared deeply for yourself or a loved one—these are times where you rose to the occasion.

Cognitive distortions tend to keep us from these memories. As we view the past, we sometimes experience a negativity bias, where we magnify failures and downplay successes. Just like the reverse bucket list activity, considering your life as a movie can help reinforce the fact that *you've already done a lot of things well.*

GRATITUDE MILESTONES CONNECTIONS
MEMORIES ACCOMPLISHMENTS
VICTORIES RELATIONSHIPS WINS

But of course, the movie isn't over yet. Just like the never-ending *Fast & Furious* movie series or endless supply of superhero flicks, more screen time awaits. So in addition to feeling reflective as you look back, you can also *look forward* and take a more hands-on approach for future developments or plot twists. It's your movie, after all.

In this scenario, you get to direct the rest of the movie from here on out. Of course, there are constraints, just as real movie directors have to deal with budgets, studio executives, picky actors, and so on. It's up to you to deal with the constraints however possible while making the best movie you can.

This thought exercise encourages you to actively shape your life story, make conscious choices, and embrace your role as the architect of your own narrative. *What happens next in your movie?*

Special Days for the Highlight Reel

For the third part of the book, we're going to build on the foundation from the first two parts. Once you're aware of how cognitive distortions create a false sense of urgency—and once you understand that not everything you start needs to be completed, nor does everything need to be done with excellence—you can take a deep breath and reorient your approach to living. That's why the movie analogy can be so helpful. You're editing the movie of your life in real-time, and there are plenty of scenes still to come.

When I started thinking about the movie of my life, a couple of patterns emerged. First, I wanted more highlights—special moments that I could imagine being placed in the extended trailer. For a long time, I had a series of built-in "highlight generators" I could count on. I always had a trip planned to a far-away place. I was also starting lots of new projects and working with a team to produce a big annual event that was filled with challenges.

But then my life shifted during the pandemic, like it did for so many others, and I began to travel far less. We ended the event after ten years, as some of the team members moved on to other things.

I also turned into even more of a creature of habit and routine. I published a podcast episode every day for more than five years, and I also had an exercise streak of more than 1,500 days in a row. Accomplishing these goals meant ordering my life in a certain way—and for the most part, this ordering worked well. I followed the general framework of simplifying my life in order to focus on what seemed important.

Still, I had to admit that I'd become too rigid and structured. The movie of my life was getting boring. The script needed a touch-up.

In a movie, the writing and directing team will often purposefully choose to create scenes that raise the dramatic tension. Highs are higher, lows are lower. This is done to tell a better story—hopefully one that's still reasonably true to the characters' lived experiences, just edited in a way to make viewers follow the narrative or feel a particular sequence of emotions.

For me, I wondered: How could I edit my life in a similar fashion?

• • •

One day, I went on a long walk—a very long one, at least for me. There's a restaurant about twenty miles north of my home that serves delicious cornbread. That morning, I made a dinner reservation for 7:00 p.m., then left my apartment just after lunch. I wasn't sure I'd make it the whole way, but I did. I arrived at 7:09 p.m., six hours after leaving and celebrated by eating a large pan of cornbread (normally meant as a shared appetizer for the table) all by myself.

I took an Uber back and enjoyed passing many of the places where I'd been walking for hours. During dinner and on the ride home, I thought: *This was definitely a special day!* I couldn't remember a time in my life where I'd ever walked so far.

And yet it wasn't that difficult. The hardest thing was simply deciding to do it. The whole thing seemed a little silly a first, setting out with a small backpack and walking six hours for no particular reason. Once I settled in after an hour or so, however, it was delightful.

More special days like those—that's what I wanted as scenes for my movie. They didn't always have to take up half the day or even involve strenuous activity. They just needed to be different enough to stand out.

Your Movie Has More to Reveal

Remember, some scenes of your life's movie have already been filmed. Many more, however, await production. Think of the Sylvia Plath metaphor about the fig tree I mentioned earlier in the book, where all the figs fell to the ground, unchosen and spoiled. What if, instead of a tree of future regret, you saw your life as a tree full of delicious memories? Some are chosen and some are passed over, of course, but to even have access to so many figs in the first place is an embarrassment of riches.

When you consider painful memories of your life's movie up to this point, you might find yourself thinking:

That was a rough time in my life, but I'm stronger because of it.

I'd probably make some decisions differently now, but I did the best I could at the time.

I wish that relationship hadn't ended the way it did, but I'm still grateful for the lessons it taught me.

You might even end up deciding: *I feel so fortunate to have had these scenes in my movie.*

• • •

When you feel like you have no control over your future, or when you feel overwhelmed in the day-to-day of countless choices, take a step back to reconsider the movie of your life. Yes, in some ways the answer to time anxiety is radical acceptance—acknowledging that you can't control everything—but if surrender is the first step, the next one is to move toward making more intentional choices.

In my case, I wanted to *increase the proportion of meaning in my life*. I wanted more memories. I wanted the highlight reel from the movie of my life to be even longer than all the *Fast & Furious* movies put together. (A daunting ambition, of course.) And I wanted to appreciate the ordinary moments much more.

These are achievable goals. Instead of thinking, "There's too much I haven't done. I've made mistakes and missed my chance," I wanted to believe, "Everything has brought me to where I am now. The best is yet to come."

I encourage you to try out this perspective for yourself. You, like me, can do so many things. Living in this time of history allows us more access to choice than anyone who's ever lived until now. And yes, as I've mentioned a couple of times, that fact can be overwhelming. But it's also awesome, beautiful, and filled with potential.

Thinking about your life as a movie—one where you're the director—can help you make key decisions. You can enhance the highlight reel by pursuing more special days (or simply deciding that more days will be special). You can pay closer attention to the ordinary moments that comprise each day, week, month, and year.

You can move away from simply letting your life unfold to taking a more active role in its unfolding. What happens next? What scenes remain to be developed and seen?

PRACTICE

"What Is Special About This Day?"

ASK YOURSELF A SIMPLE QUESTION TO BUILD AN ARCHIVE
OF SPECIAL DAYS AND MOMENTS.

Anxiety takes on many forms, but one opposite of anxiety is
mindfulness: feeling present and attuned to what's happening
right in front of us. When we feel anxious about time, we lose
track of what's special. (Sometimes, we even realize we're missing something special while it's happening, and this knowledge
makes our anxiety worse.)

So just as you learn to practice questioning how you spend
your time, start paying attention to some of the ordinary magic
that occurs every single day. Remember this:

**There is ALWAYS something special about
every day.**

As I went through the year while writing this book, I started asking myself *what was special about each day*. I did this in the
evening, looking back on the hours that had passed.

Try it for yourself, and don't overthink it. Just identify one
thing that was unique or different enough in your day to stand
out. If you really can't think of anything at all, or if you just feel
dissatisfied with your answer, it probably means you need to do
something different tomorrow.

What is special about this day?

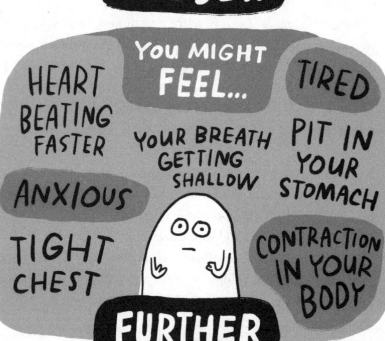

19

The Real Problem
Is We're Going to Die

TIME FEELS SHORT FOR A VERY NATURAL
AND LOGICAL REASON.

In an early chapter of the book, we looked at how our perception of time changes as we age. Simply put, when you were a kid, you thought of time differently than you do now.

Something else happens as we grow up—not to everyone, but to many of us. We don't all experience this change the same way. Some people never notice it at all. For those of us who do, however, it signals another big change in our perception of time's passing. It happens when we learn we are not immortal.

In other words, at some point we discover that we're going to die.

I know how this might sound. *Of course* we know that we won't live forever. *Obviously,* that's how life works. Yet many people are content to live in a way that is completely oblivious to this fact. It's only when they are forcefully confronted with their mortality that they begin to take stock.

This is true even though the awareness of our own mortality

can be very helpful in showing us what really matters. Thinking about death can make our lives better.

In *The Three-Body Problem*, the first book in a science fiction trilogy by Chinese author Liu Cixin, the protagonist experiences a strange set of circumstances that draws him into an investigation. One of the early clues that something is wrong comes after a morning he spent taking photographs around the city. The protagonist, Wang Miao, is an amateur photographer who works with analog film, developing it in a darkroom in his apartment.

On the day he develops his images, he notices a series of numbers at the bottom of each photo. The first one looks like this:

161:15:50

That's odd, he thinks. Similar numbers appear on all the other photos, but the numbers themselves are slightly different. Later that day he loads another roll of film, shoots more images, then develops them—to the same result. The numbers still appear, and this time he notices that the numbers are descending in a consistent order:

161:06:22

161:05:48

161:02:11

That's when he realizes the sequence of numbers isn't random: it's a countdown, representing hours, minutes, and seconds.

Wang Miao undertakes another series of increasingly frantic experiments, swapping out film, trying different cameras, and going digital. Each time he receives the same results, with the numbers appearing in decreasing order on every image. The only change comes when he asks his wife and child to use his equipment to take the photos instead of him. For the photos they take, no countdown appears.

Later, as he takes a drive to clear his head, he sees the countdown on the dashboard of his car. When he goes to the movies, it's displayed on the screen. It's following him!

As you might guess, the countdown is a disturbing discovery for Wang Miao. In a very short period of time—no pun intended—he becomes obsessed with causing it to stop.

Interestingly, the author never specifies what happens at the end of the countdown (some other things take place before then that make it irrelevant). Implicitly, however, Wang Miao understands that the countdown is the number of hours he has left to live.

He's terrified, and with good reason. If he only has six days left, the pressure to use the time well is surely overwhelming. The feeling is an extreme version of time anxiety.

. . .

We too have the sense of a countdown for our lives. It's not one that appears on movie screens to terrorize us, and we don't usually get to know how much time is left on it. Nevertheless, at some point we begin to understand that time is not unlimited, at least not for us. The universe may go on indefinitely, but we won't.

The root cause of time anxiety isn't that we haven't planned our day well or spent enough time with a vision board. It's that no matter what we do, ultimately we will run out of time. And as terrifying as it was for Wang Miao to experience a visual countdown of his remaining time, you could argue that most people feel the pressure even more: because we don't have a specific, visual countdown timer, we don't know how much time we have left.

With such an uncertain timeline, it's impossible to allocate a full life's worth of goals, projects, and activities. We can try, of course, but there's no guarantee the plan will hold up. As John Lennon put it in a song, "Life is what happens to you while you're busy making other plans."

The Problem of Being Mortal

Far from being irrational, the fear of running out of time is perfectly reasonable. Eventually, *we do run out of time*. Everyone dies.

There is no avoiding this fact in the end. It is our one universal experience, a shared destination that awaits us all. We're anxious about the future because the future is finite. It won't go on forever, at least not for us.

I once wrote a book about people who undertake dazzling, life-changing quests. I wanted to understand what, if anything, they had in common. Some of the characteristics I found might seem predictable: people who set out to complete bucket lists are goal-oriented, for example. They enjoy the journey as much as the destination (in fact, arriving at the destination is often bittersweet).

But something else stood out that I didn't expect: many of the people had what I described as "an emotional awareness of mortality." They were particularly sensitive to death and often spoke about it without prompting.

Sometimes this awareness came through a tragedy, like the premature death of a loved one or a close call of their own. Other times, however, it was hard to pinpoint a specific origin.

For as long as they could remember, they had been thinking about death. This pondering wasn't abstract; it was personal.

To see the difference in perspective, compare these two statements:

1. Everyone dies someday.
2. Someday, I will die.

In the second statement, mortality feels much more personal. It's not just other people who will pass away one day; it's also you and me.

The finding in my earlier book was clear: those who personalize the lens through which they considered death were more likely to pursue a series of ambitious goals throughout their lives.

Contemplating your mortality doesn't come naturally, though. While it was helpful for the people I wrote about who pursued big quests, it can also be terrifying, like it was for Wang Miao in *The Three-Body Problem*.

This, I thought, was an important clue. Thinking about death can make us anxious, or it can give us purpose. How can we have less of the former and more of the latter?

"No, thank you. I'm going to die one day."

The very first thing this knowledge of death can give you is a sense of profound freedom. Whatever troubles you have, whatever recurring worries weigh on your mind—all of it will eventually end. No matter how hard something seems, it won't last forever.

The second thing is that once you know you're going to die, you can use it as an excuse for anything you don't want to do. You have a terminal illness called life. Use this to your advantage!

When you're feeling pressured, when you struggle to break free from someone else's expectations for how you should live your life, or even if you just don't want to go to work tomorrow, the knowledge of your mortality grants you a built-in explanation for anyone who asks you for something.

Try it out for yourself!

"Would you like to come to this event you won't enjoy?"

"No thank you, I'm going to die one day."

• • •

"Can you drop everything you're doing and solve this problem for me?"

"I'd love to, but I can't. I only have a limited number of days to live."

• • •

"I noticed you were behind [on your emails, your taxes, whatever]. Can you get that in order?"

"I'll do my best, but I won't always be around, so I'm trying to prioritize."

It's the kind of thing that might sound rude or abrupt, at least when you don't usually think about the fact that you're going to die. But that simple truth is what will allow you to refocus and make bolder decisions.

The World Is Ending—What Now?

What would you do if you thought the world was ending soon or that your own death was imminent? Imagine you suddenly received some type of mortality countdown like Wang Miao in the book I mentioned earlier.

Almost everyone I've asked about this can think of something specific they'd like to do. Often, the answer relates to a person in their life with whom something feels unresolved. It's not always a romantic relationship; sometimes it's an overdue apology to an extended family member. Other times it's thanking someone who made a critical difference in their life during an important time.

Sometimes they don't want to say what it is—which makes sense, since the question can lead to deeply personal answers. Whether spoken or unspoken, however, more often than not, there is a clear answer. Something is there!

• • •

Assuming you don't get the dramatic experience of seeing a visual countdown of your time on earth, there's a simpler and less stressful way to put yourself in the shoes of someone forced to think about their last minutes to live. Simply ask yourself, "What is unresolved in my life?"

Granted, it can be a scary question to try to answer—but if you've read this far, you know that the willingness to ask and answer hard questions is a key to feeling better. Avoiding them sometimes feels good in the moment, but facing them head-on can provide lasting relief. Who knows, you might end up undertaking a whole new course of life events, one that wouldn't be possible without some introspection.

So go ahead, answer it for yourself. See if anything floats to mind and make a note if it does.

As for what comes next, breathe easy. The best next step isn't always to do something about your answer right away. After all, if a person or an idea came to mind, it's probably not a huge surprise. That situation has been bothering you for some time. You have at least three options for dealing with it:

1. **Reach out, follow-up, or otherwise take action.**
   If you're feeling motivated to change the universe (or, at least, dust off some broken communication lines), you might as well put those feelings to work. Making amends or saying something that you'd feel bad about leaving unsaid forever is a noteworthy occasion.

2. **Accept that now isn't the time to do something about it.** The alternative—and equally valid option—is to understand that sometimes things are left unsaid or undone for a reason. You might not want to rush into revisiting something that could end up creating awkwardness or difficulty.

   Life is messy, and some difficult situations we encounter may never be resolved. When you face the choice to "go big or go home," sometimes it's best to go home.

CALLING . . .

VOICEMAIL

MESSAGE

ACCEPT

DECLINE

3. **Think about your answer as you keep reading.** Like the activities in the book on paying active attention, by noticing points like this that come up, you'll begin living differently. Maybe this observation will spark something else, perhaps in a future relationship dynamic. You can't fix everything about the past, but if thinking about something that's unresolved helps you be clearer in other situations you have more control over, that's a win.

No matter which option you choose, if you're able to identity something that feels unresolved in your life, you've gained helpful information.

Use This Mindset to Make Decisions

But wait, there's more! Now let's assume you're not dealing with a mortality scenario, even a hypothetical one. (It's kind of stressful either way.) Developing your intuitive self by thinking about unresolved situations can help you make better decisions.

As I've explained, time anxiety occurs in all dimensions of time (past, present, future). However, the only dimension we can personally experience at any moment is the present. Therefore, when you're feeling anxious, any tool you can apply right away is especially useful.

When I started going to therapy, a lot of the concepts I encountered were new to me. One of the things I struggled with in the beginning of that experience was *learning to feel* as opposed to just thinking. The first therapist I saw kept asking me to describe how I felt at different times. I would answer, and she'd say,

"Okay, but that's not a feeling." I was always thinking with my head instead of feeling with my body.

Then, even after I finally understood the difference, my vocabulary was limited. I'd say things like "Oh, that felt good" or "It was bad." Pretty basic, right? At one point my therapist started to get frustrated, at least as much as a therapist is supposed to show such an emotion. "Aren't you a writer?" she asked. "Surely you can come up with more descriptive terms."

I knew she was right—but it was difficult. Learning to pay attention to the felt sense wasn't something I'd ever learned.

Closer or Further? (Toward or Away?)

Earlier in the book I encouraged you to pay attention to everything that happens during your day and consider how it feels. When you combine this technique with developing your intuitive sense, over time you'll be much better off in making decisions.

As we go through life, we're constantly moving toward some situations and moving away from others. We spend more or less time with friends and partners. We have hobbies that come and go, sometimes receding into the background for a while until reemerging as a priority. Then, of course, there are all the things that we're expected to respond to, which can be a full-time job of its own and crowd out anything else we'd like to do of our own accord.

· · ·

One of the causes of time anxiety is an attempt to manage all the things that weigh on our mind, both consciously and subconsciously. Contrary to much productivity advice, the solution isn't only to write down the things that need our response and add them to a task list. (If you've experienced major trauma in your life, just imagine how ludicrous it would be to put "Resolve trauma" on your list of to-dos. If only it were so simple!)

For an alternative strategy, try filtering every decision about spending time with a person or situation through the lens of *closer or further*. It's somewhat similar to asking, "What do I want more of and less of?" but also different because your answers won't always overlap.

Consider these scenarios:

An acquaintance calls to ask you for lunch. Pause before you agree to join them. Intuitively, how does the idea of spending time with this person feel? Would you rather move closer to them or further away from them? Once you have this information, making the right decision is easier.

Yes = Closer

No = Further

You're invited to attend a company retreat—but it's not mandatory. Like most things in life, there are pros and cons to the decision of whether you'll attend. Instead of making a list of them (this takes you away from your intuitive self), pause and consider your overall feeling about the event. On balance, do you want to engage with the retreat, moving toward it, or do you want to move away from it?

Yes = Closer

No = Further

You need to decide between two activities that take place at the same time. There's not a way to do both, and normally they're both things that you'd want to do. This is a harder choice, but you can still follow the exercise to see which choice might be better. Since you have to choose, ask yourself if your desire to engage one way or another is stronger. If so, there's your answer. *Which activity do you want to do more of?*[*]

· · ·

You can follow this approach anytime as a guide to help with decisions large and small. There are times when a more complex analysis is needed, but don't underestimate how powerful this question can be. Just think: *"Do I want to move closer to or further away from this?"*

Time feels short for a very natural and logical reason. The fact that everyone eventually dies can be a scary and uncomfortable fact—or it can motivate us to live more purposefully.

---

[*] Or which people do you want to be closer to?

PRACTICE

Think About Death Every Day

TO LIVE BETTER, THINK ABOUT THE FACT
THAT YOU WON'T ALWAYS BE ABLE TO.

Here is a life hack far more powerful than "never check email in the morning": **every day, take a moment to remember that someday you will die.** Hopefully it won't happen before tomorrow arrives—but it might. Even if the event takes place many decades from now, the fact remains that with each day that passes, you're one day closer to reaching this outcome. There's no going backward. Bob Dylan said it well: "He not busy being born is busy dying."

What do you do with this knowledge? Maybe you do nothing, and that's okay. You don't have to rush around every day rewriting your last will and testament. You don't need to hurry to the nearest bungee jumping site after realizing that you never got around to that bucket list item.

But if you live with the awareness that one day you won't live at all, you just might begin to see the world with a different perspective. Many things that seemed urgent or important now seem silly or trivial. If you start to give less attention to those things, how will you spend the time instead?

20

Hold On to That Feeling

FIND SOMETHING YOU REALLY LIKE TO DO,
EVEN IF IT SEEMS STRANGE OR UNCOMMON.

E very Wednesday for twenty years, Jan Mul of the Netherlands took a train to Amsterdam's Schiphol Airport. From there, he'd fly to another European city—often Stockholm, but sometimes Barcelona, Helsinki, or maybe Hamburg. Upon arrival, he'd spend an hour or two walking around the terminal, before boarding another flight back to Amsterdam. That was the extent of the trip: no sightseeing or souvenir shopping was involved.

Jan Mul did this almost every week for two decades—more than a thousand flights in total, all with the same rituals of selecting a window seat, looking out at the sky from thirty thousand feet, and airport-terminal wandering.

I know what some people will think when they read his story: *what a waste.* All that traveling without any real travel. But of course, those people weren't Jan Mul. For him, this weekly ritual made him happy. He liked being up in the air, and he enjoyed the sense of soft adventure he felt in flying to nowhere.

He'd also been able to build the ritual into his lifestyle. Because he didn't care about the destination, he booked whichever flight was cheapest—and because he returned the same day, the weekly trips didn't take him away from home for long.

I think of this story from time to time whenever I'm trying to decide what to do next. It makes me smile, partly because I too love traveling with no great sense of obligation to do something in my destination, but also because it's inspiring in a different way. Unlike so many people, Jan Mul knew what made him happy and wasn't afraid to pursue it. He also traveled for pure enjoyment, not as a means to some other end.

How to Find What Makes You Happy

If you want to be like Jan Mul—perhaps without flying to a random city every week and never leaving the airport—you first need to understand what makes you happy.

It seems like a very simple exercise—but if you know how to be happy, why do you feel anxious? Why does the sense of time's passing seem so overwhelming? For some of us, it's because of the belief that nearly everything we do must conform to some form of utility. Doing something that isn't in service of a clearly defined goal or relationship feels strange and uncomfortable.

Intuitively, you might have an idea of something that would make you happier, but you struggle with overcoming this belief about utility. You might need a nudge in the right direction or perhaps some help with getting out of your own way. Here's a tip: to be happier (and less anxious), *start with feeling more alive.*

"Alive" is a funny word for a feeling. You're always alive, at least until you're dead. But you don't always feel that way, right? Many days, and much of the time, you just kind of continue without feeling one way or another. You adopt the classic British wartime slogan: "Keep Calm and Carry On." That might be a good way to survive a war, but it doesn't help when you're stressed out and not sure you're spending your time well. If you keep doing the same things, you'll continue to feel the same way.

So just as you've been trying to pay closer attention throughout your day, try to notice the standout moments where the world comes into sharper focus. When you encounter moments where you feel more alive than usual, they might startle you at first. "Oh! I feel alive. Wow."

Sometimes these moments hit you by surprise. You're suddenly aware that a fresh strawberry tastes delicious. You're out for a walk and realize the sun is shining. You're having dinner with your partner or a friend, and the time flies by.

The moments could be big or small. You go to a concert for the first time in a while. When the band starts playing, you remember how much you like live music. You've missed this! It makes you feel alive. (You should do it more often.)

Perhaps the moments are exhilarating. Chances are, there are entire days when you feel alive. There are things you do that create this sense of greater awareness—and these are the things you want to notice.

When you feel this way, everything else becomes less significant. Whatever problems you have diminish in importance. They don't disappear, but they no longer take up as much space.

When you've been in a long period of sadness or depression,

these moments of aliveness can be especially noticeable. For me, a moment like this feels as though the sky is opening up. I've been feeling distressed, and all of a sudden, it's like someone has tapped my shoulder and said, "Hey, no need to be so worried. It's going to be okay. Also, look at the sky!"

To be clear, if you've been sad or depressed, experiencing moments like these probably aren't the end of those feelings. There's no miracle cure, and those feelings will likely come and go for a long time. Nevertheless, experiencing the highlights in addition to the sadness is essential. The highlights provide a break, a reprieve, and maybe even a guidepost of where you need to focus your attention more. These moments can point toward many more.

Because time is limited, you want to capture more of these experiences—and not just once in a while. Ideally, you want to feel alive every day. This is a powerful antidote to feeling overwhelmed.

Beliefs and Behavior

When you struggle with time anxiety, you might be experiencing a form of cognitive dissonance: a gap between your beliefs and your behavior. You know you can't do everything, but you keep trying—and, inevitably, you keep failing.

It's not just letting down other people that's the problem. You're also letting yourself down. You deserve better!

It's hard to do what makes you happy, usually because (a) you're not used to it, and (b) other people don't always understand it.

But if you follow the pattern of how we're stressed about what to do and we don't know how to manage everything, a logical response emerges. Because time is so limited, we should recapture and reclaim as much as we can.

For anyone who struggles in prioritizing their own happiness, know this: the person you're neglecting the most is yourself. This is especially true for anyone in a service role who especially likes to help others. And dare I say it's more common for women than men?

This isn't universally true, of course, but gender norms have often placed different expectations and limitations on men and women, which can impact their ability to pursue happiness. In many societies, women have been expected to prioritize the needs of their families over their own desires and aspirations.

Breaking out of this expectation—or at least modifying it somewhat—is hard. It's also an important key to feeling more purposeful.

Create a Memory Bank of "Alive" Experiences

Even though you intuitively know some of what makes you happy, it can be helpful to reflect on a broader set of experiences. To do this, start by making a list of times you've felt alive. These could be relatively recent memories or times from long ago.

Here's a short list of a few of my memories. I tried to jot them down quickly without overthinking it:

- Hosting a world record attempt for the most people dressed in dinosaur costumes
- Traveling through the night on a train in Eastern Europe
- Connecting with a friend I hadn't seen or talked to in a while
- Volunteering for a cause or campaign I cared about
- Solving a problem in a book manuscript and making progress

- Taking my event team to an obstacle course activity
- Speaking on a stage in front of a lot of people

Sometimes the magic comes from a unique, one-off experience (like hosting the world record attempt), and other times it comes from something you do often. For the recurring memories, my mind often goes to running outside. Not every run is magical (in fact, most aren't), but for me there's something special that occurs often enough to make the magic worth chasing.

One note: if you're making a list of your own, be wary of adding activities like "watching TV" to this list. This isn't a knock on TV—like most people, I can enjoy a good show or series from time to time. But passively watching a screen is not usually the best remedy for feeling less anxious about the passing of time. If anything, binging TV just causes more time to pass with nothing to show for it.

Once you have a list of your own, identify some repeating elements of these activities. What do some of the activities have in common? For me, they include:

- Joy
- Challenge
- Making people happy
- Creating something
- Being bold

With this list, I can see that several activities on my "alive" list connect directly to the list of elements. For example, hosting events requires a lot of hard work (and can be challenging!), but when done well, they can make people happy.

Some repeat elements aren't all about service to others. When

I was traveling all the time, it didn't really have much to do with anyone other than me. It was strictly a solitary pursuit, something I decided to do when I couldn't stop thinking about the idea. Therefore, not everything that makes me feel alive has to do with service, community, and connecting people. Quite the contrary! Feeling more alive often relates to looking within yourself, not outside.

Jan Mul's weekly jaunts were not in service to anyone. They recharged his batteries and allowed him to be more helpful elsewhere. When in doubt, remember: You want to find the things that make you feel most alive. Follow that feeling. Chase the sun.

Random Acts of Feeling Alive

For many people, the idea of flying to nowhere (and then repeating the same trip every week for twenty years!) is preposterous. If they like travel at all, they like the destinations, the people, the food, or whatever else they associate with taking a trip.

But Jan Mul's story points to an important principle: doing random things can make you happy. If you like to do something that might be considered strange or odd to other people—you might have found an important clue to making the most of your time.

I asked my readers for examples of something unusual that makes them happy. A few examples:

"I love going to nice restaurants by myself. Some people never eat out alone, but I really enjoy it. I bring a book and a journal, and I always order dessert."

• • •

"Every year I take up a new hobby, or at least try it out for a while. This year I've been into metal detecting, which definitely qualifies as weird to most people. I enjoy it, and I also like the fact that I decided to try it even though it seems strange."

• • •

"I'm trying to go on every major roller coaster in North America. There are more than a thousand of them, so it will take a while, but the joy is in the journey. I like planning my next road trip while watching online videos about the roller coasters I'll encounter."

Answers like these align with Jan Mul's weekly flight-to-nowhere habit. If it's fun for you, do it! Do more of what makes you happy, even if other people don't understand it.

• • •

On November 8, 2014, Jan Mul took his usual trip from Amsterdam airport. This time, he was accompanied by his grandson Tom, who dreamed of becoming a pilot. The trip was uneventful, as most of these trips were, at least until it took on greater significance as the last flight Jan Mul would ever take. Two days later, he had a heart attack at the grocery store and died. His life of daydreaming through European airports was over, but he'd lived well.

Whether you're struggling with your day-to-day or seeking a greater purpose (or both), feeling more alive is a great start.

There's a sense we experience when we feel most alive. Life is fleeting, and we can't do it all—so find the things you truly enjoy and do more of them.

PRACTICE

Subjective Units of Happiness

TRACK YOUR SELF-REPORTED HAPPINESS
AS YOU GO THROUGH THE DAY.

Subjective Units of Happiness (SUH) is a term used in psychology to describe a self-reported measure of happiness or pleasure. The word subjective is used because this measurement is based on your personal experience, instead of any other factor. You're the judge!

Trying it out is easy:

Whatever you do for your next block of time, rate your level of happiness on a scale of 0 to 10, with 0 being no happiness at all and 10 being the most happiness ever.

As with some of the other exercises, there's no need to do anything else; just note how you feel, without overthinking it. Try it again later, when you're doing something else.

Assigning a number to something makes it more precise. You could be happy sitting on a bench in the park or skydiving, but wouldn't one of those experiences be *happier*? (Note: answers may vary!)

Thinking about SUHs can help you understand your emotions and track how your happiness changes over time. As time goes by, some obvious trends should emerge. For example, you might notice:

- Planning a trip or activity feels almost as good as the excursion itself (this is known as the anticipation effect)

- Something that seems routine or "basic" is actually a source of joy
- Spending time with certain people does *not* make you very happy

Each observation offers a corresponding suggestion. If you notice that planning activities feels good, plan more! If something routine is a true source of joy, do more of that thing (and don't worry about it being "basic"). If spending time with certain people causes distress, maybe you should seek out fewer opportunities with them.

You can combine this activity with the concept of "more of this, less of that" where you simply pay attention and make mental notes of what you'd like more and less of. Again, do more of what makes you feel happy—and for a clue of what makes you happy, consider what makes you feel alive.

21

How We Respond to Regret Is More Important than Avoiding It

SOME AMOUNT OF REGRET IN LIFE IS SHARED AND UNAVOIDABLE, BUT THERE ARE STEPS WE CAN TAKE TO MINIMIZE THE PAIN IT CAUSES.

D ramatic movies tend to draw special attention to a few key choices the main character makes. Often, one of the most interesting parts of the storyline is how the character chooses to respond to tragedy and loss. These choices lead to before-and-after sequences: once a crucial choice is made, there's no going back. Sometimes, the character experiences sorrow or regret about a choice and spends the rest of the movie trying to undo the consequences.

Perhaps this is why so many movies (and stories in general) about time travel are so popular. Who hasn't had the fantasy of going back in time to change something? Don't we all wish we could say or do something different when we were younger?

Maybe our longing is to mend a broken relationship, something that happened with a person we loved. Or maybe we would have studied something different in college, not gone to college at all, or taken that big trip we kept deferring.

Whatever the situation is, paying attention to something in

our past we regret, or to something we might regret in the future, can be helpful.

Positive and Negative Effects of Regret

Avoiding future regret has long been a powerful motivator for me. The positive effects of asking myself "Will I regret it if I don't try?" led me to undertake projects like the quest to visit every country. After I first had the idea, I couldn't get it out of my head—and I knew I'd always regret it if I didn't try.

Thinking this way continues to influence my life years later. The long walk I took in search of cornbread is a much smaller example, but it followed a similar thought process: *now that I have the idea, I think I'll be happier if I follow up on it than if I don't.*

This is called *anticipatory regret,* and it can be a helpful tool in making decisions. But as I learned more about time anxiety, I realized that I'd also struggled with some negative effects of being so focused on regrets. Drawing on the emotion to think about the future and make active choices was helpful. *Dwelling* on the emotion for events in the past, however, was disturbing. This obsession affected my relationships, my work, and even my health.

I was good at building small businesses to an initial level, but they always plateaued as I abandoned them to focus on newer projects. My newer books didn't sell as well as the earlier ones, and I was plagued with the sense of not keeping up. A turbulent relationship I was in should have ended earlier, but it felt impossible for me to pull away. I regretted some things about all of those situations (and others, too), and I had a tendency to fixate on my errors.

I had to learn, slowly and painfully, that some amount of regret in life is natural and unavoidable. Regret is another form of loss, just as all life ultimately leads to an end. This simple fact—one experienced in some form by every living adult—is uncomfortable. We want to believe we can live with no regrets, like the message of countless bumper stickers and inspirational social media posts, but this belief sets us up for failure.

We are going to have some regrets. Learning to live with them makes us stronger, not weaker.

Making a Big Choice?
Flip a Coin—the Sooner, the Better

Economist Steven Levitt conducted a study on major life decisions using virtual coin flips to examine the impact of making significant changes. Participants who were uncertain about decisions such as quitting a job or ending a relationship flipped a coin to decide. Levitt found that those who made changes reported higher happiness levels both two and six months later, *regardless of whether the coin toss influenced their choice.*

The study suggests that people are often too cautious and that making bold changes can lead to increased happiness.

What kind of changes? Any, really, at least at first. The idea is to get comfortable with change, so that it becomes something normal instead of something unfamiliar or scary.

This is not to say that all changes are equal, or that you should change everything that's going perfectly well. But if you think about it, you might already know at least one big thing about your life that you'd like to be different.

I encourage you to focus on that thing, or those things if you have more than one. Next, think about the right time to make the change. Are some times better than others? Perhaps. But there's one lesson I've learned in many years of writing about change, as well as from hearing countless stories of readers who've made lots of changes: sometimes it's too late, but it's rarely too soon. Almost no one ever says "I wish I'd made that change later."

It's either the right time or it's overdue! Sure, there's probably some exception to the rule, but most of the time, maybe even almost all of the time, you'll feel better after making a change you've been thinking about for a while.

I asked my readers for stories of times when they'd made a big change and whether they felt it was the right time to make them. A few examples:

> For many years I considered going back to grad school to support a change in my career. The huge investment gave me pause and I had close friends recommend against it. "You don't need grad school to make a career change. Just start doing the work you want to do." True, but I kinda just wanted to go to grad school. After nearly ten years of hemming and hawing (and forgetting about it entirely for a while) I finally decided to go for it and it was the best thing I've ever done. It's definitely the change I wish I'd made earlier.

· · ·

> I wish I had met my dad sooner. My relationship with him (now two years old) makes a huge difference in my life and his. And I'm proud of my courage for finally reaching out to him.

• • •

I decided to start therapy with a gender-affirming therapist, and shortly thereafter came out and started to transition. So . . . lots of changes. And I definitely wish I'd done it sooner!

• • •

The last big change I made was to stop drinking—definitely one that I feared in advance that has brought so much relief afterward!

I thought about stories like these as I was working on this book. Like my readers, I've made a lot of changes in my life, and sometimes I've been afraid in advance of doing so—but afterward, I almost always think, "Wow, I feel so relieved."

The relief comes from accepting that a lot of things are outside our control—but also that you can find joy and purpose in focusing on the limited areas where you can make a difference, both for your life and for others.

Remember: almost no one says "I'd wish I'd made that change later." If something's on your mind, pay attention to it.

PRACTICE

The Ten-Year Regret Test

"HOW WILL YOU FEEL ABOUT THIS DECISION
TEN YEARS FROM NOW?"

How do you make big decisions? Most of us do so with a combination of head and heart (or "math" and "magic" if you prefer). We might make a pros and cons list, considering the costs and benefits of a particular course of action. Alternatively, we might proceed entirely based on intuition.

Here's a third way to do it. When faced with a choice, ask yourself:

How will I feel about this decision ten years from now?

This question helps to filter out the noise of the present moment and reduce the weight of immediate pressures that might lead to you deferring the decision. (Remember, not making a choice is making a choice.)

You can apply this question to many types of choices:

- Should I change jobs or pursue a new career path?
- Should I move to a new city or country?
- Should I go back to school?
- Is it time to commit to or end a relationship?
- Should I spend more time on hobbies that don't generate income but make me happy?

In many cases, the ten-year regret test will produce an immediate answer. But what about when your answer is "I don't know"?

Ah, so here's where it gets interesting. One thing you can do to help you decide is: focus on what feels right for the next step.

For example, if you aren't sure whether you should pursue a college or graduate school course, think about how it feels to apply for it. Based on what happens after that, you can always ask the ten-year regret question again later when you have more information.

• • •

Some ideas in this chapter, including the ten-year regret test, are based on concepts from Dan Pink, author of *The Power of Regret*. Dan also wrote *When,* another helpful book that I used for reference in Chapter 16.

1	2	3	4	5	6	7
MONDAY	TUESDAY	WEDNESDAY	THURSDAY	FRIDAY	SATURDAY	SUNDAY

8 YOUSDAY!

22

The Eighth Day of the Week

WHAT WOULD YOU DO WITH AN EXTRA FREE
DAY THAT CAME ALONG EVERY WEEK?

Many years ago, I wrote in *The Art of Non-Conformity* about
the model of thinking through an ideal day. The basic idea
is that if you're not sure what you want to do with your life, it
can help to imagine an ideal, perfect day from start to finish.
This includes everything from what time you get up in the morning to what you have for breakfast to how you spend each part of
the day—lots of big and small details.

But what I'll show you here is a little different, because there
are two big limitations to the ideal-day model: first, there's a lot
of pressure in creating it. *Whoa, I have to decide what my perfect day is? That makes me anxious!* We're supposed to be decreasing that sense of pressure with these activities, not adding
to it.

Second, what you do on a single perfect day might be a lot
different than what you'd do if you could repeat this day.

The solution to both limitations is: instead of thinking about
this single perfect day, **think about an imaginary eighth day of**

the week. This day is just like it sounds—it's an extra day that comes along every week, maybe between the weekend and the following week, or maybe midweek.

On this day, pretend that it's as though time stops. Not only that, but all of the external forces that usually occupy your time pause. No one's expecting anything from you. Also, the day doesn't have to be idyllic or perfect—it's just that the day is yours, and it repeats.

How would you choose to spend this day, not just once, but again and again—fifty-two times a year? For example:

- What could you learn in a year?
- What could you accomplish creatively in a year?
- What are the big dreams you've been deferring?

Those are just a couple of prompts that might get you thinking. Speaking of thinking, try not to *overthink* this process. Just go with what feels right at first.

If you're curious about where we're going with this, it's pretty simple: first, you can reclaim some of your time to do many of those things you hope to accomplish. This isn't just a hypothetical exercise—everything we've been doing throughout the book so far is designed to help you focus and live better.

Also, thinking this way will help you prioritize without reverting to thought patterns or neurological pathways that are overly familiar. Since you don't currently have an eighth day in your week (or so I assume . . .), you don't have anything planned for it at all.

When I asked my readers how they'd spend an eighth day of the week, responses varied (as you'd expect). Many of them pointed to introspective hobbies like playing music and reading.

Lots of people mentioned going for walks. Another common theme was the idea of spending this day with no agenda. Jen Zeman's comment on my blog explains this idea:

> The eighth day, the ideal day, for me is always one free of an agenda. No one else's agenda, nor a rigid to-do list I've created for myself. I just flow without watching the clock: casual tea time in the morning; exercise for as long as I want; read, daydream, paint, play with the dogs, whatever my heart desires through- out the day. Then end the day with reading in bed (which I do now, every day), maybe even a good movie.

If you have some ideas of your own on how you'd spend this eighth day, congratulations: you've identified something impor- tant that's missing or underdeveloped in your life. If the first thing you thought of was "I'd go for a walk on my bonus day," this might be a sign that going for a walk now would be good. Or if your mind goes to relaxing without an agenda, perhaps this is a sign that your life as it exists now is over scheduled.

What can we do about that?

What Do You Really Want?

For much of this book, the message has been "You can't do it all." Believing otherwise will only end up frustrating you. But it's also true that as you focus and live more intentionally, there's a lot you can do. These are the objectives you want to be able to devote maximum energy to.

One tip as you make this transition: what you *really* want can sometimes be different from what you first imagine you want. To get to the heart of the matter, it helps to peel back any exterior layers that are covering up your goal.

As a personal example, I once thought about taking pilot lessons. I love to fly, or at least I love being up in the air, moving between cities and watching the world go by. So when I first had the idea of learning to fly a plane, I thought it was a logical fit. The more I looked into it, though, the more I realized that becoming a pilot wasn't an ideal goal for me. It would take a long time to become qualified, and at the end of the process, all I would be able to do is fly very small planes for short distances. If I wanted to go much further (literally), it would take even more time and be much more expensive.

What I liked most about being up in the air was looking out at the clouds, daydreaming while a flight attendant brought me coffee and sparkling water—and it turns out that's not quite how it works when you fly tiny planes on your own. You have to pay close attention and keep the daydreaming to a minimum. Worst of all, there are no flight attendants offering beverages and little snack packets.

Of course, plenty of people enjoy taking flying lessons and getting their pilot's license. *Good for them.* For me, thinking about the idea taught me more about what I really wanted. What I wanted was to keep flying in my designated role as a passenger. I'm happy to relax while someone else flies the plane!

By contrast, going to every country in the world—one of my personal goals—required some hardship that most people would gladly prefer to avoid. I fully understand that 99.999 percent of people have no interest in traveling to remote places, stressing out over visas, and sleeping on airport floors (among other things), all in pursuit of what might seem like an arbitrary goal. But for me, facing those challenges was absolutely worth it. In fact, pursuing this quest was something that helped me feel more alive, a concept from an earlier chapter.

As with everything in life, you have to decide for yourself. The more you adopt other people's goals instead of choosing your own, the more likely you'll continue to be discontented and frustrated. Finding your own way is worth the effort.

For the dreams and goals you choose to value more than any others, how will you make them happen? Again, think about what you really want.

Imagining an eighth day of the week helps you identify what's truly important to you when you feel free from everyday pressures. Use these insights to prioritize your energy and make day-to-day decisions.

PRACTICE

More of This, Less of That

NOTICE WHAT FEELS MEANINGFUL AND WHAT FEELS
DRAINING AS YOU MOVE THROUGH YOUR DAY.

Earlier in the book, I encouraged you to actively question every opportunity for how you spend your time. Let's build on that: as you go through life doing all sorts of things, pay attention to how it all feels. Then, ask yourself: "What do I want more of, and what do I want less of?"

Try to get as specific as you can. Almost everyone wants more joy and less stress, but what is stressful for you? What brings you joy?

Just like with the earlier exercise, for this practice you don't necessarily have to start taking deliberate action on what you notice. Merely by paying attention to how things feel can help you make subconscious improvements.

Throughout the day, notice what you want more of and what you want less of.

23

Planning for a Year Is Easier than Planning for a Day

LONGER PLANNER CYCLES ARE BOTH HEALTHIER AND MORE EFFECTIVE THAN SHORT ONES.

You may have heard the saying, "The days are long, but the years are short." Gretchen Rubin coined this phrase in reference to parenting, as she watched her two daughters grow up. The days are full of details, with lots of things to pack in, but before you know it, the earth has made its way around the sun again.

The saying makes sense when you think of raising children and probably for other examples as well. But I've also thought of it in the opposite way: the years are long, but the days are short.

All too often, I try to cram too many things on a single day's to-do list, only to fail at completing any important items at all. The lack of progress feels discouraging and can even become a self-fulfilling prophecy: *the more I attempt, the less I accomplish*. Then I feel bad, and since I tend to revert to this pattern over and over, the cycle continues.

Yet I know if I plan well—not overscheduling myself and connecting the day-to-day with a greater, long-term purpose—over time I can do so much! Recognizing this distinction led to a core principle that I use for my annual planning session:

We overestimate what we can accomplish in a day, but we underestimate what we can accomplish in a year.

Most of us have access to lots of time, if we choose to use it well. The sum total of 365 days a year gives you a lot of runway. For me, once I started thinking about this longer time span, bigger goals became much more obtainable.

Thinking about time in this way is also less stressful. The hyperfocus-followed-by-burnout cycle experienced by people with ADHD and other neurodivergent conditions makes it difficult to be constantly productive—but, over time, we can accomplish a lot. Knowing this allows you to make progress and also to forgive yourself when you need to pull back.

Let's go back to the two problems of time anxiety. Remember, most people tend to mention at least one of these scenarios:

The **big-picture, existential anxiety,** often expressed as "I don't know what to do with my life" (lack of vision, missing a sense of purpose)

The **day-to-day pressure,** often expressed as "I don't know what to do right now" (feeling overwhelmed and stressed)

The answers to the two problems are connected. Once you know what you want to do with your life—or even just some parts of it—you can start to apply that perspective to how you spend your days. The goal is not to pack more in, but to pay attention and make deliberate choices.

The Crossroads of Dreaming and Doing

For just a moment, try something scary: fast forward in your mind to the end of your life. I won't ask you to visualize your own memorial service or consider what your friends might say about you. I'm just suggesting you imagine yourself in a place where you can think back on your time on earth and consider two things: *What are you most proud of,* and *what do you most regret?*

Chances are, you aren't going to remember most of what occupied your mind on any particular day. You almost certainly won't think about meetings or emails, or many other things that have caused you distress. Good or bad, almost all of the time you ever spent, spread across your whole life, will go unconsidered.

Most likely, you'll find yourself thinking about a few people and a few accomplishments. Perhaps you'll identify a theme or guiding value of your life. Or perhaps you'll just remember some very special moments.

Like the analogy of your life as a movie, thinking this way can instantly help you recognize what's most important to you. The visualization can be more than just a mental reset—it can also help you redirect how you spend your time each day.

We all make some big choices in our lives. During these pivotal turning points, you decide what you'll choose to do and what you'll leave behind. From there, what happens next doesn't just happen passively—instead, you go out and make it happen! Or at least, you're a big part of moving something along.

What if that time of deciding was right now?

Returning to the present, let's leave behind the memorial service and make some intentional choices.

By now, you understand that the future can feel scary because everything eventually ends. You know that adding more to your life without a plan or purpose can be unhelpful. You also know that giving up and going off the grid isn't the answer either.

You want more of some things and less of others.

So now what? Let's introduce a new principle: the connection between wanting something and getting it. Everything you could ever hope to achieve in life requires two key components. First, you need **an idea.** Second, you need to **make that idea happen.** In between the two lies everything that stands in the way—all the constraints and obstacles that impede your progress.

• • •

Naturally, most people are better at one of these things than the other. We can call the two groups dreamers and do-ers. Each group has a core strength and a fundamental weakness. The dreamers suffer from big ideas that seldom come to fruition. If they don't have a plan to handle all the distractions that will inevitably come their way, they'll likely get sidetracked somewhere—and then they feel frustrated. They had a big dream! But they couldn't pull it off.

As for the do-ers, they have a different problem. The do-ers tend to be very good at doing the wrong things. They are fastidious. They don't check their email in the morning. They're never late to a meeting. They dedicate themselves to quotas and goals.

Yet as you might have guessed, they're frustrated as well—just for a different reason. They're too busy ticking off to-do lists to think much about dreaming. They mistake efficiency for effectiveness. Producing becomes the end goal, not the means. They run the risk of becoming lost in the details.

The fundamental weakness of each type tends to follow dreamers and do-ers around. At the end of their lives, the typical dreamer might have some regrets of the road not taken or the big goal that didn't come to fruition. The typical do-er regrets something else: looking back, all they see is a bunch of completed checklists.

We Need to Be Both

You can probably see where this is going. To live the most fulfilled life—to do more of what you really want and thus reduce your sense of flailing—you need to be good at dreaming (creating ideas) *and* doing (executing them).

Most likely, you're already pretty good at one of them, but your limitation with the other is holding you back.

In many parts of life, improving our weaknesses is not always a wise strategy. We tend to be more successful by leveraging our strengths, not by trying to be average in everything.

But the "dreaming and doing" combo is one of the exceptions. You simply must learn to know what you want and be willing to take practical steps toward getting it.

If you excel in idea generation, great! You need to spend more time learning to make some of these brilliant ideas happen. Otherwise, there will always be a built-in ceiling to your ambitious goals.

On the other hand, if you're the superorganized person who thrives in bringing order to your environment, if you love spreadsheets and project-management apps—that's awesome! But if that's you, most likely you're in a similar place as I was in a few years ago, when I was good at all of those "do-er" things but still felt like something was missing. Being good at doing the wrong things is no better than being a big thinker who can't make things happen.

What if you could apply the mindset of the dreamer to the skills of the do-er? Chances are, you'd be able to *do a lot more of what really matters.*

You'll also be able to go after more of your most important goals while letting go of many of the less exciting things that hold you back. Last but not least, you can do so in a way that dials down the angst and frustration you feel about not having enough time.

I won't promise that you can live without regrets. Life is full of both joy and pain. Hard things happen, sometimes even terrible things.

But here's a truth to hold fast to: to live as joyfully and purposefully as you can, with as few regrets as possible, requires a combination of dreaming and doing.

Remember, we often overestimate what we can accomplish in a day, leading to frustration and anxiety. But we underestimate what we can achieve in a year. Longer-term planning reduces daily stress and boosts meaningful progress.

PRACTICE

Choose a Yearlong Project

CONSIDER A PROJECT WITH A YEARLONG TIME HORIZON. WHAT COULD YOU DO FOR A SMALL AMOUNT OF TIME EACH DAY THAT WOULD ADD UP TO SOMETHING SIGNIFICANT?

Longer time horizons like a year allow us to stretch out and work toward goals that feel especially meaningful as they build. As a writer, my favorite example is writing a book. You can't write a book in a day, unless it's an extremely short one. But you can definitely write a full-length book over the course of a year.

My friend Laura Vanderkam is especially fond of yearlong projects. In one recent year, she read *War and Peace*—a towering novel that clocks in at close to 600,000 words. (The average book is 10 to 15 percent of that.) Conveniently, *War and Peace* features 361 chapters, so Laura read one a day. If she missed a day, no big deal, she just caught up when she could.

You could also choose more of a "habit project," where you do the same thing every day for a year. This is a little different from something with a project cycle (like finishing a book). Some examples of habit projects include:

- Running or walking at least one mile every day for a year
- Writing at least one page in a journal every day
- Taking a photo every day and posting it on social media

- Learning a new language, a few words at a time every day
- Starting and maintaining a garden (which includes a built-in seasonal cycle!)

When you're struggling with your day-to-day, adding in goals and practices with a longer time horizon can feel comforting. What would you choose to accomplish in a year?

People often avoid
making decisions out
of fear of making a
mistake. Actually the
failure to make decisions is
one of life's biggest mistakes.

—RABBI NOAH WEINBERG

Happy Holidays!
YOU ARE CORDIALLY INVITED to a FESTIVE EVENING OF STANDING Awkwardly IN THE CORNER.

24

Weddings, Holidays, and Other Depressing Events

IF YOU SOMETIMES FEEL SAD OR ANXIOUS
DURING BIG LIFE EVENTS OR HOLIDAYS,
IT MIGHT BE EASIER TO CREATE MEMORABLE
MOMENTS ON MORE ORDINARY DAYS.

When we think about special days, we tend to think of two categories: big life events and holidays. Both of these categories can be stressful—even to the point of becoming truly distressing.

Big life events include occasions like graduations, weddings, and births. Sometimes these are great days! But sometimes they aren't. You might experience complex feelings during these moments. A new season is beginning, but that also means that another season is ending.

Even when these days live up to the hype, they can still be stress-inducing. Not every bride or groom who cries at their wedding is full of regret—sometimes getting married is an overwhelming experience that brings up a lot of emotions.

Or what about giving birth? The experience is painful and difficult for both mother and child. Some who give birth describe it as a beautiful memory. Others describe it as traumatic and painful—perhaps a necessary process for bringing life into the world but not necessarily something they remember as a joyful series of moments.

In all of these "big life event" situations, the participants are generally expected to be happy. A new mother isn't supposed to complain about the birth process, even a difficult one. Getting married? Everything about your life must be amazing, because look around at all of the single people in the world! (Yes, this is a slight exaggeration.)

This pressure around big events doesn't just come from other people; sometimes it's self-applied. "Why wouldn't I be happy to have arrived at this moment," you ask yourself. Everything in your life has been leading up to this point, so how dare you feel sad or confused about it. And then you end up masking your true feelings, even to yourself.

• • •

Now let's look at holidays. Unlike some of those big life events, holidays tend to have a habit of coming around fairly regularly.

Many people who struggle with time anxiety also experience complex emotions around holidays. When everyone else appears to be exuberant, you feel the pressure to pretend. You might be sad, worried, overwhelmed, or just stressed.

The end-of-year season in December can be especially challenging. No matter what your feelings are, you're supposed to go around acting like everything is awesome. The same is true with birthdays, or "themed" days like Mother's and Father's Day. If you've lost a parent or child—or if you didn't have a healthy relationship with a parent—you might dread the arrival of these dates on the calendar. Valentine's Day is similarly complicated for many people.

Time Is Weird During the Holidays

However you feel about designated annual celebrations (even if you love them), there's one thing that applies to us all: time is weird during the holiday season! Like it or not, *we all enter a time warp.*

In many industries, work essentially stops for several weeks during the holiday season, even when there are plenty of days when employees are still showing up. At a certain point, people start saying things like "Let's circle back on this in the new year."

Our schedule and routine changes, with or without our consent, and for many of us, so do our habits. We eat and drink more, leading to a different cycle of resolutions, gym memberships, and dry Januarys on the other side.

I don't want to tell you what to eat or how you should behave during the holidays (or any time of year). In terms of time anxiety, though, this thought is important: when we're in the time warp, our emotions tend to be exaggerated. Because of all these factors, we can experience more intense feelings—good ones and bad ones.

If you've been feeling mostly happy by the time December rolls around, you might feel happier as the season of merriment unfolds. But if you've been feeling anxious or sad, the same principle of intense emotions holds true. In those situations, your negative emotions can become exaggerated just like any others.

A Partial Solution: Find Something to Focus On

So if you're like me and holiday seasons are sometimes difficult, what do you do? For better or worse, extended hibernation for weeks or months is only an option for animals like bears and hedgehogs.

Since outright escape is usually impossible, I recommend you start by recognizing what's happening and have compassion for yourself. You don't need to share your feelings with everyone around you, but you also don't need to pretend to be joyful when you're not.

Personally, I love a good project during the holidays. It helps keep me grounded. Unlike animals who hibernate, I don't completely escape, but I withdraw to work on whatever project I have or enjoy. Looking back on recent holiday seasons, I can spot a difference in my mood and well-being based on whether I had something specific to focus on or not.

Even though I enjoy writing, I don't have to use it as a work project to help me cope with the holidays. Getting lost in a long, story-driven video game can also be fun. Granny hobbies are ideal: if you like to knit, set a goal to make five new hats or attempt a bold sweater design. The specific activity doesn't matter so much as your enjoyment of it.

Finally, you may or may not be able to reframe the holiday season as something positive (personally, I've had mixed results in trying to do this). Either way, you can continue to focus on increasing the amount of meaning in your life and celebrate special days that you create for yourself any time of year.

• • •

The idea of manufactured special days, whether through big life events or holidays, is one area where movies and real life are different. In a movie, scenes are placed to represent touchstones of progression. The director wants to elicit a certain emotional response from viewers. If we're following a story about a character's life, it's natural to see highlights from those big life events. They are stand-in scenes designed to lead the audience along.

In life, however, many of the truly special moments seem ordinary or unexpected. Far better, then, to recognize special moments on ordinary days. Many times, these moments only appear special in hindsight. But if you can increase their quantity, both in their overall occurrence and in your own recognition, you'll feel more purposeful.

It's normal to struggle during holiday seasons and big life events. Accept the complexity of emotions, choose a personal project to regain control, and create your own special times.

PRACTICE

The One-Minute Ease Break

LEARN TO PIVOT FROM FRICTION TO
EASE WITH A SIMPLE RESET.

Set a timer on your phone to go off at three random points during your day. When you hear the chime, ask yourself, "Am I feeling friction or ease right now?"

If you're feeling ease, savor it! Pause and really feel that lightness and flow in your body. Anchor it by tapping your wrist and saying "ease"—this creates a physical trigger you can use anytime to remind you of that feeling.

If you're feeling friction, use this minute to get unstuck. Stand up, shake out your hands, and take three slow, deep breaths. Then ask, "What's the simplest next step I can take to reduce this friction?" Trust the first answer that comes to mind. Now take that one small action, letting the momentum carry you forward, away from friction and toward ease.

Over time, you'll train yourself to recognize the feeling of friction quickly and learn to switch back into ease.

25

Pay Yourself First

INSTEAD OF DEFERRING YOUR FAVORITE
ACTIVITIES UNTIL EVERYTHING ELSE IS
HANDLED, FLIP THE NORMAL STRUCTURE
AND LOOK AFTER YOURSELF FIRST.

In the world of personal finance, there's a model called "pay yourself first." It refers to the practice of automatically setting aside money for your savings account and retirement funds whenever you get paid. You need money to pay bills, but if you don't prioritize saving, some people argue, it will never happen. Even if you happen to be extremely disciplined, putting a savings plan on autopilot will free up your mind to worry about other things.

That's fine and well when it comes to saving money—but might there be a way to apply the model to spending time? What if we made "fun" less of an afterthought and more of a priority?

As I've said, I didn't write this book out of academic interest. I wrote it because I was struggling with my difficulty in coming to terms with time. If affected my life almost every day.

At some point, I realized I connected "leisure" with a form of reward for work. Productivity-wise, this can be an effective strategy. I would tell myself that if I finished a task I was dreading,

I'd reward myself with some kind of treat. Finish writing my daily one thousand words? Now I could play my video game for half an hour. Did I run enough miles for my long weekend run? Great, then I could eat pancakes.

Well, that's a decent productivity hack—and by now, you know that productivity hacks can mask greater problems. I didn't need permission to stop work early. I could eat pancakes whenever I wanted, at least in moderation.

So I started playing games more—sometimes in the middle of the day! It felt strange at first, like I was sneaking away—even though I work from home and set my own schedule. It's not as though the work police were going to bang on my door and tell me to get off the couch and move to my desk. But that's really what I felt would happen. *Strange. Unfamiliar. Uncomfortable.*

After twenty-five years of working for myself, I had to learn it was okay to do something that had no connection to output or a work product.

Learning to Spend Time on Leisure

If you, like me, struggle with prioritizing fun, most likely you just need some practice. Try this:

1. **Pay yourself first.** Use the personal-finance idea and plan your days more around what you like to do and less around your obligations.

   Again, not everyone can do this all the time, but the point is to think about what's possible. Whenever you can, schedule your responsibilities around your other interests, instead of the other way around. Why should your best time go to someone else?

2. **No need to justify it.** When I started prioritizing my hobbies more, I felt like I had to explain or justify it—even though no one else cared. The weird guilt I felt in playing video games in the afternoon gradually subsided, but it required a real adjustment in perspective.

   This need to justify how you spend your time is common. "It's my monthly treat," some people say about something special they like to do. What if this special thing is part of your daily routine? It's your life, so choose wisely.

3. **Combine planning *and* spontaneity.** There are two types of leisure activities: those you plan for and those you just do. Sitting down on my couch to play games in the afternoon doesn't require much planning. It's also not something I want to do all the time. Other activities require some sort of advance commitment. You need to buy the concert ticket or make plans with a friend for dinner.

   Most likely, you'll want to incorporate a combination of both types: planned activities and spontaneous fun. How do we do that?

Start With Planning Something

Let's take travel as an example. Some people like to plan *a lot*. I know someone who makes a detailed spreadsheet for her annual vacation, down to line items denoting meals and outings for every day. I respect the process—I just don't live like that myself.

A person who plans everything out all the time might need to relax a little. Some of the best experiences are spontaneous and unplanned—don't be afraid to get out and about without a detailed agenda.

That said, my problem came from the lack of planning. I didn't want to be pinned down, so I didn't plan anything at all, and on many trips, I didn't end up doing much of anything. Similarly, I didn't "go out" much while not traveling. Except for my morning run, it wasn't unusual for several days to pass without me leaving my apartment. Often I'd work through the day, pausing for the run or to lift weights in the gym in my building, and only emerge to pick up food from a delivery driver in the evening.

During my run or brief errands, I'd blink as I looked up at the sky and out at the city. *That's right,* I'd remember. *There's a world out there.*

Aware of my tendency to either (a) fly around the world and do nothing, or (b) stay at home and do nothing, I began reforming my habits. As a traveler who never made plans, I started making them. For every trip, I tried to plan at least one excursion or designated outing a day. I could still be flexible with the rest of the time, but this excursion or outing was the way I'd be certain that something would happen.

In New York I went to a comedy show, something I wouldn't normally think of doing. When a friend offered me a ticket to interactive theater, I didn't say "I'll think about it." I accepted the kind offer and had a great time.

Looking further out, for two years in a row I'd thought of going on a sailing tour of Croatia, but when I finally went to book it, the tour was sold out. The third year, I decided to do something wild and crazy—I made my booking many months in advance.

Then, on the home front, I started buying tickets for concerts and other local events that were at least a few weeks away, and sometimes longer. Making plans was hard at first—every time I went to buy a ticket, I'd think, "But I might not be able to make it." I tried to overcome my resistance by remembering the adage about booking plane tickets: "The confirm button never disappoints."

In the worst-case scenario, when I booked something and then couldn't make it, I simply wouldn't go. Sure, the ticket would be wasted, but that wasn't the end of the world. The trade-off of an occasional burned ticket was more than made up for by the other activities that worked out.

As I started making more specific plans for free time, I noticed two curious effects. First, as a planned event approached, I'd often start second-guessing it. I'd question if it would be "worth it." The introvert in me started dreading a social experience.

Perhaps most of all, I'd worry about the time I'd spend at the event. "Is it really the best use of my time to take a neighborhood tour," I'd wonder. I could use that morning to work on book edits, or (always the old fallback!) try to catch up on my neglected inbox.

The second effect? Almost every time I went to an event or activity, I'd be glad I did. When I made quick notes in my journal those evenings, inevitably I'd think back to those outings. Even if the activity hadn't been amazing, I liked that I was trying new things instead of just working more.

Time anxiety often comes from feeling like we're not doing enough—but paradoxically, doing more of what we enjoy can be the cure. Give yourself permission to prioritize fun and watch how it changes your entire outlook on time.

PRACTICE

The Two-Adventure Weekend

PLAN ONE BIG ACTIVITY AND ONE MINI-ADVENTURE
FOR AN UPCOMING WEEKEND.

It's good to prioritize free time even on work days, but it's also true that most people tend to have more of it during a couple of days each week. Whatever your weekend looks like (even if it falls on different days than other people's do, or if it only comes around a couple of times a month), try setting a goal of having two adventures each weekend, one planned and one more spontaneous.

What's an *adventure*? The word adventure is a broad term that could mean a lot of things, from going to an activity or exhibit, taking a class or workshop, going rock climbing, or simply exploring a new place.

Think of it like this:

Having an adventure is an <u>exciting</u> or <u>unusual</u> experience that is often associated with <u>novelty</u>, <u>challenge</u>, and <u>exploration</u>.

The underlined adjectives are clues to what your weekend could look like: adventures should be something a little different than what you usually do.

As noted, I suggest that at least one of the two adventures should be planned in advance. The second adventure can be spontaneous—but if you find spontaneity to be difficult, plan this one, too.

Why not just live your life and pursue soft adventures all the time? Well, some people can (and do!) live that way. But most people can't or won't. In the midst of so many competing demands, we struggle with putting ourselves first. Then, we use our free time more passively, instead of putting in a small amount of advance work that will result in much more rewarding experiences.

You schedule work meetings and doctor's appointments, so do the same for things you enjoy. You'll do more of them this way, and you'll have the added benefit of anticipation as well.

Bonus tip: enlist a companion in at least one of the adventures.

26

Instead of Leaving a Legacy, Learn to Live Well

A WAY TO FEEL BETTER, AND A BETTER WAY TO LIVE.

The nonstop travel I undertook for a decade was linked to something deeper. For at least that long, thinking about legacy was a primary motivator for me. I wanted to be someone, to build something. I connected this motivator with a means of production: if only I wrote enough books, produced events for enough people, started enough projects . . . then, well, I'm not sure what I thought would happen. I guess I thought that, cumulatively, these things would add up to a sum greater than the parts and I could look back and say, "Mission accomplished!"

Undoubtedly, there's some ego involved with thinking like that. But ego isn't the whole problem with the achievement-oriented mindset. It's good to be proud of what you've done and who you've become—I believed that long ago and still do. The greater problem is believing in its permanence.

• • •

As I began to find my way out of the worldview that had governed my thinking for so long, I started to consider my goals through a different lens.

Around this time a friend sent me a video on why men don't need therapy. She'd received it from a family member who, not surprisingly, was pushing back on her suggestion that he might want to think about talking to a professional. The friend wanted my opinion, so I dutifully watched it.

In the video, the expert (spoiler, a former therapist who started a coaching program) went through various reasons why he believed that therapy and most mental health models were unhelpful for most men. One of the things he said stuck with me: "What men need is to build a legacy that will endure after they're gone."

Watching it, I felt frustrated. *This is not helpful advice!* I thought. You are setting yourself up for failure if you insist on an outcome you have no control over.

Yet what the speaker said also felt familiar. After all, for years I had believed and said similar things. (Not the part about half the population not needing therapy, but the part about leaving a legacy.) I too had believed that the purpose of life was to leave something behind, in some important-sounding but vague way.

Maybe this was part of my problem? What I saw as highly positive—the desire to build something that would endure—was contributing at least as much to my daily sense of frustration and angst.

The pressure that we somehow "must" use every minute well creates an impossible goal, an endpoint that sets us up for repeated failure. What if we don't use every minute to its utmost potential? Surely the world won't come to a stop, because ultimately our part in it isn't that important.

In the end, I thought, attempting to build a legacy might just be another way of trying to stem the tide—to stop the natural progress of time, as well as a universe that tends to go on existing perfectly fine without us. Remember, the ocean is endless. Also, the ocean does what it wants. It doesn't adjust its behavior to suit our schedule or preferences.

One day, we're going to die. Until then, we have all the time in the world.

The Better Way: Focus on Living Well

"Legacy building" as a motivation is different from the concept of legacy itself. Here's the distinction: undoubtedly, some people do leave a legacy, but it's hard to purposely build one.

So what can you do instead?

For me, I realized that what I wanted most of all was to *live well*. This goal still comes with pressures and stressors, of course, but of a lesser kind.

Living well doesn't mean living hedonistically, caring only for yourself. Living well involves caring for yourself *and* others, recognizing them and helping them along wherever possible.

Maybe this is where the legacy part comes from: not what you build or leave behind, but simply the logical result of a life well lived, one that is generous and kind and helpful *and* without continuously deferring your own dreams. One that practices setting boundaries, both out of respect for others and for yourself.

Living well is a virtuous goal. Best of all, it's achievable—it's something we can do. As little control as we have—we can do this!

We can do it today, in the way we react to the many things that come our way. We can push aside much of the incoming firestorm, gathering only what we need for the few things we can do well. We can take the time for simple pleasures.

We can do all of this with the knowledge that what we do won't be perfect and other things will be undone. Such is the price to pay for being human.

We can live well as we plan for the future, full of the knowledge that our plans may end up being sidelined. Sometimes that happens! We're not responsible for the final outcome—we only need to make the best possible attempt.

Old Habits, New Changes

As I come to the end of the book, I'm not going to tell you that I've solved everything that was troubling me. Even as I wrote these chapters, I struggled. Some days I drank more coffee than was good for me. I felt the pressure of finishing a book that was about the pressure of finishing.

My inbox management is somewhat better now that it was before, though it's far from perfect and probably always will be. I'm sorry if you've written to me and I haven't replied. *It's me, not you.*

But I wanted to write a book that would change me, in addition to (hopefully) being helpful to others. What's changed for me is that I have self-awareness, perspective, and some acceptance. I can recognize the cognitive distortions that lead me to feeling so distressed. I can understand that while striving is important, it's also important to understand that the ebb and flow of life is a natural cycle.

The phrase that kept coming back to me over and over was: *focus on what you can do, not on everything you can't.* When it comes to getting things done, focus on the list of completed items more than the unfinished one. The unfinished list will always remain in that state, because there will always be more to add to it. But the completed one grows as well, and that's something to be proud of.

Honestly, I realized, if I can do only that and nothing else, my life will be infinitely better.

And so I offer this advice to you as well. What did you do today? Did you get out of bed? Did you complete a single task? If so, celebrate that. Take the win. Maybe you can catch your breath today and do more tomorrow, if that feels good. Or maybe you can learn to live more freely, not stressing out as much about all the things you haven't done.

. . .

As I let go of some expectations and obligations, I felt better. I still don't post consistently on most social media platforms. What's changed is that now I accept this fact for what it is instead of seeing myself as a miserable failure. When I look at the social media accounts of friends who do a much better job at posting than me, I try to think, "Good for them!" instead of "I am terrible." They've chosen to prioritize their social posting. I've chosen other things.

As I tried to increase the proportion of meaning in my life, I found myself making different choices. I planned trips to visit friends, with no other agenda but to see them and catch up. I'm sure some of them thought this was strange at first, since I'd always had a project to talk to them about. But the time I spent with them was *good*.

I spent more hours every day writing, which seems logical enough but had become difficult over the years. It's astonishing how easy it is to have a career as a writer without doing much writing—but at least for me, that never felt right. What did feel right was getting back in the routine of making daily progress on a book or other assignments. Everything else, or at least many other things, could wait.

In fact, letting things wait, or refusing to give in to the illusion of false urgency, is a common theme in how I've changed. Other things I've learned are:

- Not everything we start needs to be finished. (It's okay to walk away.)
- Not everything needs to be done with excellence. ("Do things poorly" is a perfectly acceptable strategy much of the time.)
- Though it sometimes seems that the world operates at a single, high rate of speed, we can deliberately slow down how we engage with it.

It wasn't a time-management tweak or productivity hack that brought me to this point. I still had the same number of hours in the day, just as I'd always had and the same as everyone else does. But in choosing to engage more in writing and creative projects—without worrying nearly as much about the outcomes—I felt better.

Do I still want to leave a legacy? Well, sure, but I'd also like to live forever. While I'm at it, I'd like to win the Powerball lottery, preferably without spending any money on a ticket. I'd like the ability to fly or become invisible. Most of all, I'd like the ability to turn back time, or at least pause it for a while. But since none of those things seems forthcoming—and in fact, since legacy is just as much outside my control as any of the other wishes—I have chosen to refocus.

So I encourage you to do that as well: to be proud of all that's brought you thus far. To do more of what you can. And to stop trying to do it all.

Take the Chances You Are Given

We have a certain amount of time in which to choose. Some of us have more than others, both in terms of overall length of life as well as the amount of freedom we have in which to spend it. We could dwell on this fact for a long time, or we could use what time we have to do what we can.

You were once told you could be anyone, do anything, have it all—and even though it sounded good, you always suspected that something was wrong with this idea. You were right to be skeptical. How could you really have everything? Even children learn to understand the concept of impermanence. Instead of keeping up the facade as adults, we should embrace the joy of careful selection. By letting go of much, we can hold tight to the few things we choose.

You suspected there wasn't enough time for everything—and you were right. This knowledge can be your advantage, your secret strength. If you keep it close to your heart, honoring its truth, it can bring you peace in the midst of overwhelm.

It can help you remember that it's okay to not do it all, because in fact such a goal is impossible. (And trying to do everything is what is stressing you out. This cycle will not magically resolve itself, so you need to step in and put it to rest.)

But just as there is not time for everything, there is still time for so much.

There is time for risks, leaps, and adventures. There is time to advance, retreat, regroup. The days that lie ahead of you are filled with possibilities. There is time for big ideas. There is still time for dreaming.

There is time to walk outside and look up at the sky. There is time to celebrate the miracle of everyday living.

There is time to get closer to the people you love. There is time to love someone new.

There are still figs on the tree, waiting for you to select them. Above all, there is time for choosing.

Truly, there is time for a life well-lived.

If you're reading this right now, there's still time.

AFTERWORD:
THIS BOOK IS FOR YOU

A short note to the reader who has made it this far.

A writer always hopes that their book will be helpful to readers. And so I offer this book to you, the reader who's come this far.

Know that your experience with time anxiety is shared with many others around the world. Sometimes, the naming of a shared experience helps us all to feel better, or at least to know that we're not alone.

There are no magic solutions, but hopefully you know by now that *you are not powerless*. There are things you can do to make today better than yesterday and tomorrow better than today. I hope you'll do some of them, and modify the suggestions I've given however you need to in order to make them work for you.

Lastly, if you've enjoyed the book, I'd be very grateful if you would share it with anyone you think might benefit from it. Personal recommendations make a huge difference in helping books and ideas spread.

Most importantly, take care of yourself over there.

CHRIS GUILLEBEAU

Special thanks to:

David Fugate | Talia Krohn | Emily McDowell | Leah Trouwborst | Paul Whitlatch

Readers and friends of *The Art of Non-Conformity* and *A Year of Mental Health*

MANIFESTO

1. Leave ten minutes earlier than you think you need for every appointment.

2. Learn to discern between real and imagined deadlines by asking, "Can this wait?"

3. Create a reverse bucket list to celebrate past achievements instead of fixating on future goals.

4. Use "time decluttering" to remove unnecessary commitments from your schedule.

5. Practice the art of no-guilt communication with friends to maintain relationships without pressure.

6. It's impossible to keep up with everything, so avoid the temptation to try.

7. We overestimate what we can accomplish in a day, and underestimate what can happen in a year.

8. Not everything you start needs to be finished.

9. No one ever says, "I wish I'd made that change later."

10. To live better, think about death every day.

INDEX

ABOUT THE AUTHOR

CHRIS GUILLEBEAU is the *New York Times* bestselling author of books, including *The $100 Startup*, *The Happiness of Pursuit*, and *The Art of Non-Conformity*, which have been translated into more than forty languages and sold over one million copies worldwide. During a lifetime of self-employment that included a four-year commitment as a volunteer executive in West Africa, he visited every country in the world (193 in total) before his thirty-fifth birthday.

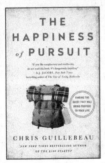

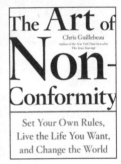